THE SHAWS MULTIPLIED

DORIS HOWE

Copyright 2023 by Doris Howe

ISBN: 979-8-9888980-2-3 (Paperback)
979-8-9888980-3-0 (Ebook)

All rights reserved. No part of this publication may be reproduced, distributed, or transmitted in any form or by any means, including photocopying, recording, or other electronic or mechanical methods, without the prior written permission of the publisher, except in the case brief quotations embodied in critical reviews and other noncommercial uses permitted by copyright law.

The views expressed in this book are solely those of the author and do not necessarily reflect the views of the publisher, and the publisher hereby disclaims any responsibility for them.

Olympus Story House

CONTENTS

THE SHAWS MULTIPLIED 1

"EDUCATION WAS ALWAYS A PRIORITY" 4

THE MULTIPLICATION STARTED 6

MEMORIES OF THE SHAW FAMILY IN ORDER OF BIRTH
FROM TED ANDERSON. 9

SOME SPECIAL MOMENTS BY DETTA
(SHAW) SAFRANEK 11

TED ANDERSON'S PERSONAL STORY 15

GOD GIVES SECOND CHANCES 24

GOD TURNED BEAUTY FROM ASHES BY MARY FRANCES
(SHAW) HUNSE 31

MY "BEAUTY FROM ASHES" STORY—DORIS HOWE. 36

RUTH SHAW VICKERS. 40

MARY AND VAL: (AGAIN) 56

TECHNOLOGY'S ADVANCEMENT 58

FARMING WITH IRRIGATION 62

LEARNED FROM GREAT, GREAT GRAMPA
HARVEY YEAMAN 65

MEMORIES FROM JANET 68

TERRY COLWELL. 72

DORIS AND JANET'S VACATION 75

ALOHA 79

VALETTA'S MEMORIES 84

MARY KAY (HUNSE) COLWELL 92

REDEMPTION FROM WATER FEAR 95
A PUT DOWN CAN HAVE LONG
LASTING, NEGATIVE EFFECTS...................... 101
TESTIMONIES FROM THE DESCENDANTS 106
WORLD TRAVELING 110
CONCLUSION...................................... 115

THE SHAWS MULTIPLIED

A long time desire to chronicle the lives of Douglas and Amanda Shaw and their progeny has become a reality. From stories from the remaining cousins this book has become a reality. Douglas, Amanda, and their ten children have departed this earth. But, at last count 133 descendants are living. This book is dedicated to all of them as well as those yet to come.

To those of you who contributed, thank you. You may never know how your story impacted another's life. As you read this book, I pray that your imagination will kick in and you will see between the lines and what you do see will bring very pleasant memories. I want everyone to enjoy reading the book and come out of that experience with a newer sense of roots.

This book is a brief history or roots of the Shaw family. I have said that we ALL have stories. Even though you may not have known these grand parents, Douglas and Amanda Shaw, you will be blessed and get a real connection to them by all the stories from several generations back. The research has introduced me to not just our grandparents but to aunts and uncles and cousins in a more personal way. It will do the same for you.

You will see stories of how God has worked in various situations in the lives of this family. This book is really all about God and how He worked in the lives of our ancestors, parents, and us. This book will show the Goodness of God in your lives as well as in my life. My prayer is that when you come across the stories of the works of God in our various lives as well as the lives of family members, you'll be

The Shaws Multiplied

reminded of how God worked personally in several situations in your life. As you read, see God more clearly in the stories and KNOW He is not a respecter of persons. No matter your personal lives, God has been, is now, and shall work even Great things in your future! The purpose of this collection is to give those who are left and those yet to come a feeling of roots.

A positive element of this Shaw family with all the siblings and their spouses that I want to emphasize is they all accepted one another as true siblings. It was an unconditional love that is not found in many families, especially extended families, today. Each member of the family whether "blood" or "in- law" was accepted with that kind of love in spite of the differences in personalities, living styles, or occupations. This love often showed up in teasing ways or availability when a need presented itself. These characteristics make me proud to be a descendent of the Shaw family. I pray the same is for you. I endeavor to continue that closeness and unconditional love in my descendants.

The only picture I have of Amanda's dad is of him and his wife. He has in his hands a huge Bible. I have since learned a whole lot more about him. Not only was he a "traveling" preacher; but also his character and personality and accomplishments have painted a more expanded picture of him than we saw in that one photo. The roots we have of this ancestor are traits that have led to the majority of the third generation cousins to embrace Christianity.

Additionally I'd always known Douglas and Amanda prayed for the salvation of their family and friends. So, from both sides of Doug and Mandy, the inheritance took root and established fruit—an explanation of the legacy we all enjoy in Christ.

Your contributions have made the history more real. I've tried to fill in some holes with information from my meager research as well as my life. My goal is to show positive aspects of these ancestors that will bless you and maybe even help to make you stand taller because of your personal roots and the influence each has had to develop your strengths. Hopefully you'll see and understand from whom you got your interest in farming, or military, or politics, or teaching, or writing, or hospitality, or service, or career, or law enforcement, sewing, crafts, or your work ethic: honesty, strength of character, sense of humor, or Christianity. I am sure you can come up with other traits that you have seen in this family tree that I have not mentioned.

Even if you did not personally know Douglas and Amanda Shaw, and are farther down-line from them than your parents, I pray you get a connection that you did not have before this book came into your possession.

Think of this project as an adventure and it will give each of you a bigger picture of the family than you had before this project became a reality.

"EDUCATION WAS ALWAYS A PRIORITY"

March 22, 1885

Douglas Shaw, my dear grandson,

Your very kind and thoughtful letter of the 9th was received a few days ago and I hasten to answer it for fear I might neglect it too long, for you will have to go into the country if you work on a farm, and you might not get my letter after you leave the city.

I am always glad to hear from any of my people and more especially from you as you are the only grandchild who has ever written to me. I can see a marked improvement in your last letter. The penmanship and spelling are better. When I was of your age, I got Webster's School Dictionary and when I would write a letter I always had it at hand to see how to spell any doubtful word. In this way I practiced at home. Then I taught school, which also helped make me a good speller until, if I do make a mistake, it is the pen that does it.

You have the foundation now. You can gain a great deal of knowledge by reading at home during your leisure hours. Here are some books I used to read and study at home. First The Holy Bible, then the History of the United States, then a Geography. I always kept the geography handy so that I could locate any proper name I came to in my reading. I also had a school-work on Philosophy. Oh, how much you can learn in that about the laws of mechanics and motion. Chemistry, like philosophy, taught me a great many useful things about the composition of matter and things in general. Many have supposed I had a college education, but I was self-taught. I was always fond of grammar, and became quite a grammarian. Most of the grammar I learned at home. However, I got started with the interest in grammar at school.

Your brothers and sisters are now separated and will have to fight life's battle unaided by a loving mother. Oh how much there is in the influence of a fond mother. But my paper is full. Do not forget me wherever you go.

Your affectionate Grampa, G.P. Harvey Yeaman

Eliza Yeaman, the wife of Harvey who wrote this about his wife. Both of them died young and left children.

Eliza was the daughter of David Orr and Rebecca Stephenson. She was born in Union County, Indiana, January 24, 1817, and died near Mount Pleasant, Iowa, May 13, 1859.

She was an affectionate and faithful wife and mother; ever engaged in seeking the comfort of her family.

She professed for many years to having passed from death into life, having experienced the new birth in Christ. Only a few days before her death she expressed her assurance of grace and salvation. Her only wish to live was for her children.

Her final departure was without a struggle or a moan; with her senses to the last. She asked for a drink of water, which she took. She held the glass in her hand only a few minutes before she died.

A lady, Mrs. Pitcher, was fanning her. Her last words were "Not quite so hard." In five minutes or less she was gone.

A tumor on her right breast seemed to be the main cause of her death. Signed, Harvey Yeaman

"Every house is built by some man; but He who builds all things is God." Hebrews 3:4

THE MULTIPLICATION STARTED

FAMILY TREE OF DOUGLAS D. SHAW AND AMANDA ELLEN (RICE) SHAW:

Douglas was born in Knox County, Illinois to Nicholas and Eliza Shaw on January 10, 1866. He passed away at his farm home in Pine Canyon. This community is located about 9 miles Northwest of Callaway and about 15 miles south and east of Arnold in Nebraska. He died on January 14, 1943.

Douglas came to Nebraska in 1877 and made his home on Cliff Table until July 13, 1890 when he married Amanda Ellen Rice. As young married folks they made their home on the Will Beckler farm for three years. It was then that they moved to DeMoines, Iowa. Doug was a plumber and worked at that trade for eleven years. They then moved back to Nebraska and purchased the home in Pine Canyon where they resided the remainder of his life—37 years. He was a contractor and builder and practiced that trade for many years. There are a great number of homes on the Cliff Table that have his trade mark in houses, barns, and many other buildings. He was a tireless worker always honest and giving the other person the benefit of extra hours worked. He would walk from Pine Canyon the 3-5 miles to work on a Sunday night and walk back home on Saturday night. After World War I, his three sons returned from service. Two of the service boys, Ora and Clifford and another son, Joe, worked with him at carpentry work.

Amanda Ellen Rice was born of Sarah Ann Mullen Rice and William Jasper Rice on September 13, 1872. She had two sisters: Martha Frances Rice and Mary L. Rice. She had four brothers, Edward, James Riley, Charles Elmer, and John C. Amanda came with her parents to Custer County April 1887 from Missouri by covered wagon. The family took a homestead and a pre- emption claim on which they made their home until she married Douglas D. "How beautiful are the feet of them that preach the gospel of peace, and bring glad tidings of good things." Romans 10:15.

William Jasper Rice's father, Erastus Rice served as a soldier in the war with Mexico. Grampa Rice, Amanda's father, enlisted in Iowa to fight in the Civil War when he was nineteen. He passed through the Atlanta campaign and the raid through Georgia. He took part in the important battles of Nashville, Tennessee as well as numerous minor engagements.

Later in his life he represented the Columbia Fire Insurance Company. He was active in politics and was for many years justice of the Peace of Cliff Township. He served on the Republican Central County Committee. At the primary in August 1918, he received the nomination of his party as a candidate for the state legislature.

He was also an ordained minister of the church traveling as a circuit rider for several years before his death. He was a great influence in his community. He was always ready to extend a helping hand to the poor and the distressed. He was a deeply thoughtful man, with a keen insight into human nature and an analyst of moral and political conditions. He passed away November 25, 1930, at the age of 86. Family members' lives were greatly enriched by knowing him.

Amanda's mother, Sarah Ann Mullens Rice was born December 27, 1842. She lived to age 85. She was a pioneer of the finest type. She bore a brave part in the events over a period of forty years. She was a tender and affectionate parent, a faithful wife, an excellent neighbor and a loyal friend.

The Shaws Multiplied

"Trust in the Lord with all thy heart; and lean not unto your own understanding. In all your ways acknowledge him, and he shall direct your path." Proverbs 3:5-6

MEMORIES OF THE SHAW FAMILY IN ORDER OF BIRTH FROM TED ANDERSON

First born was Nellie. I didn't get to know her or her family. They lived in Iowa and folks didn't travel as much then as we do now. I do remember hearing that she had a set of twins and a couple of other children.

Curtis married Mae, He was the first son born to Douglas and Amanda Shaw. I spent a few days with them in their Compton, California home where they entertained me. More details are here quoted.

Here is quoted a letter Curtis wrote from Camp Kearny, California on June 15, 1918 while he was in the Army.

"Dear Folks, Really have been so busy that I just couldn't get time to answer your letter which I received a few days ago. This leaves me as well as usual and do hope that these few scribbles will find you the same. How is every body and every thing? I hope fine! Have you any melons yet? Or is it too early? I guess it is. There are lots of melons on the market here, of all kinds, and pretty cheap, 2 cents a pound. This sure has been a long lonesome old day for me. I stayed at home today. But believe me, I am going to town next Saturday or Sunday if I can get a ride. Have you heard from Ora lately? I haven't heard from him for about six weeks. I guess that he hasn't much time to write. I hope that his knees are all right by this time any way. And Clifford. I

The Shaws Multiplied

haven't heard from him for a long time either. I have been wondering if he was still at his original unit.

"I got another nice bunch of pretty horses in Saturday. Twenty head, black as coal and weighing about 1300 to 1700 pounds—a nice size for artillery and caissons. We got a nice large bunch of rookies in the other day—about 6000 of them. Part of them are real old slackers and won't do a thing without there is a man over them with a loaded gun. There have been about 40 of them cut their throats with a razor and one shot himself with a little old gun that he sneaked in with him. Another one jumped in front of an ambulance that knocked him cold. Outside of a few getting sick by not eating anything, they are all right, I guess. That is how the "native son" feels about it.

"I have a picture of myself. I will send you one of them. It isn't very good, but you can put it in the chicken coop and it will keep the coyotes away. Well news is scarce and my fingers are getting tired from writing. Will have to close for this time. So. Bye. Bye. From the Sergeant, Curtis B. Shaw." It shows some of his personality as well as that Shaw sense of humor.

From some research that Shirley Shaw/Hayes found: 115 AM TR means 115 Munition Train. It seemed that Uncle Curtis trained war horses to pull the ammunition wagons. He was in the famous 40th Division at Camp Kerney, California, now called Miramar. It was also called "The Sunshine Division." Uncle Curtis did see action in France at the same places Uncle Ora would have seen action. However they did not connect in France. Uncle Curtis's main job would have been to keep the infantry supplied with ammunition from bullets to large munitions. He was living in Colorado at the time he volunteered for service. The part of his division that involved horses came home after World War I. Most of the horses were slaughtered to feed German POW's and French civilians. Who would have thought?

"We know that all things work together for good to them who love God." Romans 8:28

SOME SPECIAL MOMENTS BY DETTA (SHAW) SAFRANEK

U ncle Ora and Aunt Zella had a son, Vernon, and a daughter. Detta. The daughter is remembered for the many kind things she did for her Aunt Margie. She has such a great family. She has worked to keep the relatives in touch. Their son, Vernon, is remembered for his ornery streak. He got me on their Shetland pony before he put a corncob under the horse's tail. It was a short painful ride.

When Grandma Shaw got the family dinner, the cousins had fun playing. I remember some of us got stung by the honeybees.

When Grandma was older, we took her to Callaway to get her groceries. When Grandpa was older, he picked pretty rocks from the gravel and put them in buckets. He still found beauty in the rocks. He liked to tease the grandkids. A favorite trick was to leave a few drops of water in the dipper when he got a drink. Then he would put those drops of water on the head of the nearest, unsuspecting grandchild. Once, Doris decided to pay him back. Only she did not leave just a few drops of water in the dipper. She left it half full and poured the entire contents on Grampa's head. She thought it unfair that she got severely punished for her "pay back."

Grandma liked poetry and I, Detta, do also. A copy of a poem she wrote in her grief from losing their son, Joe.

In later years when the family came to visit and there was a need for a dinner, Aunt Mary had the dinner. It didn't matter how busy she was. She came to the door, all smiles and gave everyone a hug. Cousins always had fun. Some went to Devils Den. Later Ham and our kids and Doug and Greg liked to go to Aunt Mary's and Uncle Val's house too.

Aunt Margie was a favorite aunt also. She was a wonderful cook and could make almost anything. She and I used to trade some patterns for crafts. When she was older, I would go see her. She was so happy to see me and would always give me a hug. One of the last times I went, she showered me with pictures of all my Grand parents that I had not seen before. She let me make copies and send them back to her. I loved all my aunts, uncles and cousins. My girl cousins were like sisters that I never had.

Uncle Clifford and Aunt Mary, Erna and Ed used to come on the train to Broken Bow. Mom would fry her pheasant or chicken that was so good. Dad always had a big patch of melons. We had a great time.

Dad's army record: Ora was born October 1896, at Valley Junction, Iowa, and died at the Veterans hospital in Grand Island at the age of 70 years 10 months, and 14 days after a lingering illness.

Ora came with his parents to Milldale, Nebraska in 1904. He attended rural school in Pine Canyon. He enlisted in the Armed Forces at Grand Island, Feb 3, 1918, and served in World War I. Two brothers, Curtis and Clifford joined with him. Curtis and Ora served in Europe. Curtis was transferred to California. Clifford, it is told, lied about his age saying he was 18 when he was only 16. However, because Clifford was so young, the army gave him a 'desk" job during World War I. Ora served in World War I, Co.F 7th Infantry. He fought in six major battles in France and Germany. He was wounded, but did not want to go to the hospital. However, they let him ride in the Wagon. He told us he was in the army for 3 years.

Ora said that he wanted to find his brother, Curtis, over seas, but did not. However, he did find a friend from Arnold. I, Detta, look forward to seeing all these smiles in Heaven some day.

> "I will instruct you and teach you in the way you shall go: I will guide you with my eye." Psalm 32:8

Next in line was Uncle Clifford and Aunt Mary. Their daughter, Erna updated us here;

My parents, Clifford C. Shaw and Mary Tabor, were married May 2, 1925, in Chicago, Illinois. I, Ernestine, came along exactly two years later on May 2, 1927. My brother, Edward, was born December 5, 1928.

My dad was a locomotive engineer for the Chicago and Northwestern Rail Road. He worked mainly on the west side of town. We always lived within walking distance to his job. We did have a car. However, it was used mostly once a week to take my mom to two or three groceries. During those Depression years it paid to be frugal with my dad's income. Grocery shopping was one way my mom found to bargain hunt and help the money to go farther. Many of my mom's friends were bargain hunters as well. They often would share with one another knowledge of the grocery specials that were available at the various markets.

My dad was a typical Midwestern "meat and potatoes" man. But we ate a combination of that plus the Bohemian style, roast pork, dumplings and sauerkraut. My mother was a wonderful cook.

Mom and her family came to the USA in 1903, when she was 9 or 10 years old. I remember the wonderful times we went to see Grandpa and Grandma Shaw. We would often get to visit many of the other relatives on those trips. Being a city girl I had been protected from the things that my cousins on farms were allowed to do. It was exciting for me to jump from the top of the barn onto a pile of hay below. My mom would have had an attack if she knew of that or any number of other things we did.

After graduating from high school in 1945, I attended junior college and then worked in down town Chicago for the New York Life Insurance Company. Later I worked for Household Finance.

Now I sing in the church choir, print Braille books, and go to extensive Bible studies. I belong to the local ladies barbershop chorus.

The Shaws Multiplied

We sing at local affairs, for the hospital, and for churches. All of this keeps me quite busy— something I wouldn't change. I love it.

I married Herb Lund in 1957. My first daughter, Christine Marie was born in June of 1960. My second daughter, Barbara Ann was born in September 1961. In 1972, we moved to southern Missouri where we owned and operated a small resort. I am sorry to say that that marriage ended in divorce. After that I worked in the hospital in MT Home in 1977. I moved to Mt Home in 1982. I worked there until I retired in 1992.

I married Ed Schultz in 1994. We had seven wonderful years together. Chris died in 1996 at age 34. She left three children, April, Brittany, and Michael. They are all single at this writing. Barbara is married to Rex Lewis. Their three children are Emily, Erin, and Madison. On November 19, 2011, I became a great grandmother to Dominic Canella.

Even though I have some Muscular Degeneration, I still enjoy puttering around on the computer. It helps me stay in touch with "long lost relatives." This book will serve to connect us again.

"His compassion fail not they are new every morning: Great is thy faithfulness." Lamentations 2:22-23.

TED ANDERSON'S PERSONAL STORY

Theodore Leigh (Ted) was born January 23, 1929.

These are his words:

Marjorie and Henry were my parents. They had 4 children—Bob, Ted, Margilu, and Jim. My mother was a strong person. She worked at the Arnold Hospital before she was married. She enjoyed cooking, baking, sewing and crafts. She made her home a home for her mother (Amanda) for a few years. Amanda (Grandma Shaw) was a gentle and frail lady. She died in the Broken Bow Hospital. The last time I saw her was in that hospital before I left for the Navy. My mother gave me sound advice. She told me at an early age, "people may do you dirt, but you don't dare let them rub it in your face."

My Dad was also a strong person. His father (Pete Anderson) died when Henry was 17. It was then that dad became head of that Anderson household. He taught me by example "Hard work and Honesty." His craft was being an excellent and respected mechanic.

Bob worked with our dad as a mechanic for three years before he joined the Army. He was a helicopter Mechanics Instructor as he got an Aeronautical Engineer training from St. Louis University. Another special time for Bob was when he worked with Warner VonBraun—the German Missile Scientist from World War II.

The Shaws Multiplied

After that his work took him to Italy where he worked for the Chrysler Corporation setting up the Jupiter C. Missile. He died in a car accident in the mountains in Italy while on his way to work.

I, Ted, was born on the Emma and Pete Anderson Homestead between Arnold and Gothenburg, the second son of Henry and Marjorie Anderson. I graduated from Arnold High School in 1947. After high school, I worked as a meat cuter for the Watson Grocery in Arnold.

In 1950 I joined the U.S. Navy and spent 42 months on a destroyer as a chef.

Maybe my experience with meat cutting gave me an edge to get this duty. I knew good cuts of meat even though the military is not known for its nourishing "mess."

One week-end during my navy service waiting for the official discharge, I visited Frank and Mable Shaw and their two daughters in their home in California. They were a quiet couple. Daughters Shirley and Linda were typical little girls at that time. Frank worked for the Railroad. It was after Mabel died that Frank and Shirley came to Nebraska in his camper. We were all out at our Johnson Lake cabin where Frank brought my mom to see us. Frank liked to travel with his camper. I believe that visit was after my dad had died.

In 1954 I was discharged from the Navy. I spent a few days with Uncle Curtis and Mae in Compton, California before heading back to Nebraska. I remember their home being modest and comfortable. They welcomed me and we enjoyed the visit together. Uncle Curtis was a big and out going person. Uncle Curtis was on the Police Force during World War II. This was a career that lasted 25 or 30 years. He was in the U.S. Army during WWI. During the Korean War he was a Security Officer at the Long Beach Naval Base. Mae was outgoing and a good hostess. They drove me to downtown Los Angeles to show me around. They both came to Arnold to see Grandma Shaw when she stayed with our family. The family enjoyed a picnic at the Arnold Park with a large group of Shaw decedents.

After the Navy experience I enrolled at Kearney State College for a pre- dental course and received a BS degree. Doris Hunse introduced me to her sorority sister, Shirley Johnson, while at Kearney. Shirley and I were married in 1956.

I was accepted at University Nebraska Medical Center in Lincoln where I received a DDS (Doctor of Dental Surgery) in 1961.

Our children are Shari, Todd, Terry, and Lori. We have seven grandchildren. I had a private dental practice in Lexington from 1961 until I retired. It was then that we moved to Lincoln. It was there that I became a clinical instructor in Pedodontics at the University of Nebraska Medical Center College of Dentistry.

My Shining Star is my little sister, Margilu. As a family we spent a lot of time with Margilu and family over the years. They lived in rural Gothenburg area and we were in Lexington. Our children were close in age and enjoyed each other. Our children were able to experience farm life—animals, dogs, cats, fields, and garden. When they were little they were surprised that Aunt Lu had potatoes in the ground. We enjoyed their sweet corn and they liked our cherry tree. A fun family time happened when we picked corn to freeze and picked the cherries for pies and to can.

Both of my parents were deeply saddened when Bob died in a car accident in Italy and only three years later (to the month) Jim died in a construction accident in Arnold. With Bob and Jim both having lost their lives at early ages, I regret not having them with whom to grow old.

"For we will surely die and become like water spilled on the ground, which cannot be gathered up again. Yet God does not take away life, but He devises means, so that His banished ones are not expelled from Him." 2 SAMUEL 14:14

The sixth child in the Shaw line was Joe. Here is part of the obituary found in a local paper at the time. "JOE SHAW, a 20 year-old son of Mr. and Mrs. D.D. Shaw of north of Milldale. Joe died on Friday November 20, 1923 from the bite of a certain species of wood tick found in Montana and in some other sections of the country. The young man had just returned to Nebraska from Montana and

The Shaws Multiplied

was attacked by this illness, which is almost always fatal. The funeral was held at Cliff Table on November 23, 1923. He was survived by his parents: Douglas and Amanda Shaw, and his brothers, Curtis, Ora, Clifford, Jesse, and Franklin. Sisters who survived Joe are Nellie, Marjorie, Mary, and Ruth.

A NOTE FROM ME TO YOU

I think about you often.
And I'd write you every day.
But here seems so very little
That seems worth while to say.

It either rains or doesn't
It's either hot or cold.
The news is all uninteresting
Or else it's all been told.

The only thing that matters
Is the fact that you are there
And I am here without you
And it's lonesome everywhere.

I think about the way you smile,
And I recall your touch.
And tears come all the while,
And I miss you very much.
Written by Amanda E. Shaw
after the death of one of her loved ones.

"Blessed are they that mourn: for they shall be comforted." Matthew 5:4. Cousins who I know of who are going through grief from the loss of a child are Shirley Shaw, Jacquie Shaw, Ernestine Shaw, Valetta (Hunse) Delahunty, me, Doris (Hunse) Howe and others I don't know of. Our Gramma Shaw is a good example of how devastating the loss of a child can be. It is so out of the ordinary. Our kids are always supposed to out live us. I have learned a lot about grief as I have walked through it. Also, I have learned how to minister to these young unmarried pregnant girls who go through grief when they place their babies for adoption. Grief comes as a result of any loss.

Some time ago we attended a seminar regarding grief. I learned a lot at that meeting. One of the best things a person can do for her/himself is to talk about it. Of course, one needs to carefully choose who to talk to about it. Probably what helped me the most through my grief was to talk about it. I jokingly said, "I'd meet a stranger on the street and say, let me tell you about my son who was killed." I didn't know at the time that what I was doing was probably the best thing I could do to heal.

Another thing I learned is that most folks do not know what to say to someone who has gone through a loss that deep. They generally say dumb things in their ignorance. So, if folks have said "dumb" things to you concerning your loss, just know that they meant well. They just didn't have a clue about what to say.

I recall a few months after Joey's death. I was in a department store in Phoenix. I saw a friend who was also shopping. We, as families, had boys the same ages. We had been in their home for dinner as all our boys played in their back yard swimming pool. Likewise, they had all been in our home for a similar experience. This friend looked rather sheepish as she saw me that day. I just went up to her and began to tell her the story of Joey's death—in detail. After all that, she said, "Doris, I am so glad you came and talked to me. I saw you, but was at a loss as to what to say. I didn't know if I should ignore you or pretend that I didn't see you. But your talking about it made me comfortable. Thank you."

As mentioned earlier, it is my contention that Val Hunse died of a broken heart 3 days after grandson, Joey, was killed. A sideline here, Amanda and Douglas Shaw had 10 children. The story we had heard growing up was: A son, Joe, died while in his early twenties of Rocky Mountain Fever caused by the bite of a sheep tick. It is

The Shaws Multiplied

thought that Gramma Shaw didn't ever "get over" that loss. (I do not ever remember seeing my gramma laugh.) Anyway, the night after Joey's death, cousin Harry Jensen as well as Valetta, both reported that they had received calls from Val in his concern for me at the loss of a child. I know he was remembering his own mother-in-law's grief with the loss of her son. Val was concerned that perhaps I would not get over the loss from the death of my son. The day after these calls, my dad, Val Hunse, died. I still have concluded that it was a broken heart that killed him.

It took me some years before I was ready to do a scrapbook for Joey's memory. I had done one for the other two kids and even my three grand children. So, it was time to do Joey's. That proved to be very healing for me as well. Maybe writing your thoughts about your child's death or doing a scrapbook would be helpful for you. What I call Joey's eulogy follows:

A eulogy for Joey Howe.

When you had the opportunity to go to Austria for a year, you had a couple of excuses for not going. I remember one being that there would be no care for Max, your dog. I agreed to walk him each morning, which I did. So that excuse did not work. Then there was something about being on the "gravy train" for another year. Somehow that got settled too.

We wanted your trip to be a real adventure. So we routed you through London. There you were to stay at a Youth Hostel. I remember that you had Joe Mike's "body bag" duffle. It was loaded. You had heard that you could sell Sears Roebuck catalogs for $20 each so you took at least one. Then you had all your ski gear and clothes for the year. When you arrived at the Hostel you said that the European male travelers thought you were somewhat over loaded. They each had one back pack.

The next leg of your journey took you on a Hover Craft across the English Channel to Paris. I think we gave you a day in Paris. From Paris you got on the "Oriental Express" train ride to take you into Vienna, Austria. After the last stop prior to Vienna, a couple approached you and asked if you were Joe Howe. You said that all this time you were hoping not to look like an American. Here were complete strangers who seemed to recognize you. As it turned out they were the mom and dad of the family were you were to stay for that year. They were looking ahead and knew how crowded the depot in Vienna would be and pictured the difficulty of finding you among the masses. So they got on the train at the stop just prior to Vienna. They figured they could locate you easier on the train than in that depot. We always thought that was a very special, thoughtful thing that they did for you. And a welcome that made you feel that the year would be not just an adventure, but a very special time with good folks.

When you got there, you and Tommy, their son, overlapped a month. Then Tommy came and stayed with us in Phoenix. When you returned from your year, Tommy still had a month before he was to return to his home. So, you "brothers" got to reconnect here.

After your death, I packed up a box of your old jeans for Tommy as we had heard that American jeans were hard to find in Europe. I had written a note along with the package saying, not only were these jeans that you would have liked for him to have, but they were also "worn out," an added benefit.

Just as the time when you went to Mexico for that summer and you had informed the family that you didn't want to hear any English while you were there; the same thing was true in Austria. You were pretty well prepared with both languages before your trips. In both cases I had heard that it wasn't long before you could converse and even tell jokes with the natives, regardless of their dialects. You had said that you didn't want the natives to know that you were American/English speaking because they would want to try to speak English to you. You could not understand their English.

With your "gift" of languages, I had visions of you using those languages and making a huge impact of some sort around the world.

I remember when you were under a year old, when we would put you to bed, we could hear you practicing the words you had heard during that day. I think words always felt good tripping across your tongue, the sign of a true Linguist.

The Shaws Multiplied

Joey part two:

Joey was a "visionary" and had a spirit of an entrepreneur like his sister, Janet. In his last letter he described an idea for a unique "Wash-a-teria." In our last phone conversation he was talking about possibly working with some folks in a lunch/sandwich shop in preparation for perhaps opening one of his own in the future. My last words to him were, "You have all the time in the world."

Two weeks before the accident, Janet and Joey had a conversation about death. He said that he wanted to be cremated and his ashes spread on the Pacific. The two of them said that they did not want the other one to cry if one went before the other. When we went in to view Joey's body, I said, "This is not Joey. This is an empty shell. During Joey's life he was SO alive." Janet was crying so hysterically, she kept saying, "I told Joey that I wouldn't cry. I promised him I would not cry." All I could say is, "It is all right. You go right ahead and cry. He understands." Janet was almost hysterical with her sobs. She was angry that I had insisted that she come and view Joey. For years she said that she could not get the picture from her mind of Joey's body on that table.

Three months after Joey's death I had a dream: Joey was sitting in the passenger seat of a car that someone else was driving. He was looking at a newspaper. I was in the back seat with someone else. I didn't know the other 2 people who were in the car. As I noticed Joey reading the ads in the newspaper, that was currently dated, I said to my companion, "We must be in a time warp because Joey was killed 3 months ago." The 4 of us drove to a ski resort that had one of those ski runs that are steep. The skier just lets go and skis very quickly to the bottom of the run. When the skier gets to the bottom of the run he jumps off the end. I think the competitor who jumps the farthest wins the gold medal.

At the top of this run, Joey was the only one of us 4 wearing skis. He came over to me and kissed me on the lips. In the dream I felt his rough, chapped lips on mine. (He often had rough, chapped lips.) He then turned without a word, and skied down the steep run. As he got to the end of the run, he jumped and disappeared. That was the end of my dream. I interpreted it to be the "good bye" we hadn't had prior to his death.

Joey was Joseph Howe 8 in that many generations. Over the years we heard remarks like, "One can surely see that he is his dad's son." Granted even cousin Joseph Christian Howe (one son out of 5 brothers of Hap Howe) along with the other Joe Howes had that family resemblance.

Two days after Joey's death Grampa Val (Doris's dad) died of a broken heart in his concern for her, a mom losing her son to death. Two days after we took care of Joey's remains, we were sitting in Gladys's Catholic Church in Arnold Nebraska for Grampa's funeral. Then at the cemetery the priest said, "I will pray with you; but before I do I want you all to recall the characteristics of Val Hunse that you admired. Then I want you to ask God to help develop those characteristics in you."

When I began doing that, I'd think of one and see Joey had that same trait. As I went through each characteristic, I knew Joey had that same one. So even though Joey certainly <u>looked</u> like the Joe Howes in the family, many of his traits definitely came from the Hunse side of the family. He was definitely <u>my</u> son also.

"The Lord shall guide you continually." Isaiah 58:11

GOD GIVES
SECOND CHANCES

JEFFREY DOUGLAS HOWE
After an absence of five years and six weeks after I changed my prayer for Jeff, he called me. The new prayer was, "God do whatever it takes to bring Jeff to you." Within a month of that long, over due connection, Jeff came to Texas to stay with me. Confirmations were lining up for this "Prodigal Son" to be welcomed into my home.

He said as he crossed the border from Arizona into New Mexico with all he owned in the U-Haul truck, he felt stuff being released from his shoulders.

Jeff had been diagnosed with diabetes 2 ½ years earlier, but had not had much medical care. He was on insulin shots daily and a large dosage of high blood pressure medicine. And his left foot was quite swollen.

For the first six weeks I continued to push him out the door with applications and his resume'. No job came forth. When I talked to God about Jeff's job search, I felt God say, "Don't worry about the job. I've got that covered. You concentrate on his salvation."

On November 14, 2012, Jeff described it like this. "My foot swelled up like a melon and burst." I took him to the hospital. It had to be amputated below the knee. The poison and infection had crushed all the bones in his foot and was affecting his kidneys and liver. Bottom line: God had brought Jeff to Texas to save his life. He was given a second chance at life! And there is no sign of diabetes and the blood pressure has returned to just a bit above normal. Help is coming from many sources and Jeff has a great attitude about it all. His patience is rubbing off on me!

Initially, God let me know that I was to be the instrument to help Jeff unite with God and accomplish that new prayer. I feel that my job is to continue to love Jeff unconditionally, continue to expose him to the truth, and continue to pray for him. My prayer need is that I won't be judgmental or pushy, and that Jeff will see in me something that he wants—the Lord. I need to be the roll model of that kind of parent. "As for me and my house, we will serve the Lord."

Jesse Shaw

Uncle Jesse and Aunt Frances came next. I, Ted, took my mother to Montana for Jesse's funeral, her first airplane ride. As she was riding in the plane and looking out of the plane window, she said, "It sure is a big world, isn't it?" I remember Jacquie and Doug for a fun time when they came to Nebraska for a reunion. Like the other Shaw brothers, Jesse became bald in his late 20's. He walked with a cane when we saw him at some family reunions at the Pine Canyon farm. The story was that he fell off a wind mill and hurt his leg. Valetta said that she heard a different version of his limp directly from Uncle Jesse. He said he was working on a power line and was struck by electricity. Two things happened. He hurt his leg and his hair, instead of standing on end from the electricity, fell out and never grew back. The senses of humor are evident in all of the Shaw family. Jesse's wife, Aunt Frances, was known as a favorite aunt because of her vibrant personality. She enjoyed life and had a hearty laugh.

FROM DOUGLAS SHAW (Uncle Jesse and Aunt Frances's son)

My father came to Montana to work for Uncle Curtis in his construction company building houses for the people who lived on the irrigation project. (This is another example of the closeness of the siblings.) Jesse worked for Uncle Curtis until work slacked off.

He then went to work for Martin Olson who later became his father-in-law. He married Martin's daughter, Frances Adair Olson. Jesse drove a bus and went to work for the Sunriver Electric Co-op.

The Shaws Multiplied

He worked there until 1942 when he was electrocuted. He fell 55 feet and landed on his back breaking almost every bone in his body. They said he would never walk again. But with the Shaw determination and God's help he not only walked again, but started working at the school in Fairfield teaching Industrial Arts and Auto Mechanics. He drove the school bus and kept the busses in repair. Jesse and Frances had three children: Jacquelyn Louise Shaw, Martin Douglas Shaw (known as another Doug Shaw), and Jesse Jerome Shaw. Jacquie married Charles Hanson and that marriage produced two children: Carl Martin Hanson and Charles Douglas Hanson. They divorced. Jacquie married John L. Carlson. That marriage produced two children: John L. Carlson and Kimberly Carlson. They lost their two boys to different causes. They live in Choteau, Montana.

I, Martin Douglas Shaw "Doug" married Diane R. Groot. That marriage produced three children: John Martin Shaw, Lincoln James Shaw, and Darcy Lynne Shaw. We lived on a homestead, farm or ranch. Mom (Frances) called it the farm and dad (Jesse) called it the ranch.

Jesse Jerome Shaw (Jere) Married Treina Bural. That marriage produced two girls: Becky Lynne Shaw and Angie Shaw.

Doug says, "I remember Grampa Shaw had a glass eye. I couldn't figure out how he could remove it. It took a while. He also had a rough beard. He would rub our cheeks with it. A kid never forgets that.

Uncle Ora came to Montana. He and Dad (Jesse) trapped and shot coyotes— lots and lots of them. He later had Aunt Zella come out. She didn't like living in Montana. Uncle Ora even built her a new house. But, to her, that wasn't the same. She missed Nebraska so they went back. Dad, Jesse, asked Ora why more folks didn't move to Montana from Nebraska. His answer was, "They aren't smart enough." When they left, I, Doug, really missed them.

We live only about 25 miles from the Rocky Mountains. Growing up, we went to the mountains a lot to picnic or just to hike. One time we were snowed in for two weeks. Dad was snowed out. At that age, two weeks seemed like an eternity. We wondered if Dad was ever going to come and get us out of the snowdrifts. He did come get us and brought supplies. Our faith was renewed.

When I was about six, Dad and I went to Hemingford on the train. We got in late. Dad got a guy out of the bar to take us out to Aunt Ruth and Uncle Cecil's farm. Gramma Shaw was there. We stayed there two days before catching the train to Broken Bow. Gramma Shaw went with us. Uncle Ora met us at the depot. We stayed with Uncle Ora and Aunt Zella for a few days. From there we went to Arnold to visit Aunt Margie and Uncle Henry Anderson. On that same trip we spent some time with Uncle Val and Aunt Mary. I went to school with Mary Kay. I met a couple of kids— Gary Jacobson and Larry Nelson. We played together and had fun as six-year-old kids do. Aunt Mary was teaching school at a country school. Our visit came at Christmas time. So Aunt Mary put me in the Christmas program at her school. I was too old to play the part of Baby Jesus and too small to play the part of one of the Kings of Orient. Maybe I became one of the Shepard boys for the play. My acting career never got off the ground. Guess there were no talent scouts there at Aunt Mary's Christmas program. A few days later we got on the train and went back to Montana.

In later years when I was a junior in high school, we got a new kid in school. I got to talking to him. Guess what!! His name is Gary Jacobson from Arnold, Nebraska. We renewed our old friendship from that trip when I was six years old. After high school graduation, Larry Nelson also moved to Fairfield. We three became lasting friends. Today we are like brothers. It's a small world.

"You need to get outside and get the stink blown off of you." Mary Hunse when our attitude needed an adjustment.

Ted's information continued:

Next in the Shaw family was Mary Shaw Hunse. She married Uncle Val. Aunt Mary was always there to help and encourage my mother. She checked on both my parents every week. Val was a good friend to my dad. Aunt Mary loved to travel. It was said that she always kept her suitcase packed just in case someone was taking a trip. She wanted to be ready in case they invited her to go along. Valetta did a lot of work with Detta and Margilu to keep the Shaw Reunions going. Valetta and Tom allowed me to take care of their dental needs as did Mary and Val. I mentioned earlier that Doris introduced me to my wife, Shirley.

EDITOR'S NOTE:

Since these are my parents, I have much to add in more detail in other portions of this book.

Throughout the reports from the family, it has been noted that Mary had a gift of hospitality. His seems like a likely place to put some thoughts about that gift as it was passed down the line.

"After a large meal, one can always eat ice cream. It melts and fills in the cracks." Mary Hunse.

"Y'all come. It's a party." Doris IT IS A GENERATIONAL GIFT:

Mary Shaw Hunse had a gift of hospitality. Any excuse and she would open the doors of their home for a family reunion. Coming from a family of ten children, there were often sisters and brothers and their spouses announcing they were coming to Arnold. Many of you have your very own memories of such gatherings. Maybe it started way back on the farm of Grampa and Gramma Shaw in Pine Canyon, Nebraska outside of Callaway.

When I recall those gatherings, they would start with a vision of the three of us girls crowded in the back seat of the Buick and trying to get comfortable as we drove into the night from Chicago to the farm. It seems we always left on a Friday evening—after the work week for my parents. My dad made his living driving a truck long distances, so the drive through the night was "small potatoes" for him. A night's stay at a motel was such a foreign idea that riding all night was "normal" back then. I probably had never even seen the inside of a motel until after I graduated from college. Back to the crowded back seat of that car. We were so excited about the reunion and reconnecting with the cousins that we had not seen in at least a year, that we probably could not have slept through that drive even if there had been more space in the back seat of the car in which to stretch out.

Probably the picture that will always be etched in my mind is one of all the uncles "chewing the fat" as they took turns cranking on the ice cream makers. No ice cream has ever tasted that good since.

I recall, also, that the brothers'-in-law had a love and a closeness to one another as the flesh brothers.

As kids, I remember we cousins catching grasshoppers (there were always plenty of them) and putting each on a stick. Then we roasted them. Don't remember where we got the blaze or why we didn't start a huge fire. However, I also don't recall that we ever were tempted to taste the roasted delicacy. Years later I was reminded of our time when I saw roasted grasshoppers on the menu in an elite restaurant. (UUUGGGHHH)

Another picture in my memory was of us catching frogs. We cut them open, stirred the insides some and sewed them back up with red thread. Maybe we thought that we might find a bigger frog with a red thread incision hopping around the following time when we got together for the next reunion. Maybe this was the ground work starting for one of the cousins to go into surgery and/or dentistry as a profession.

As the years went by and many of the family members of the Shaw family descendents were scattered over the various states, whenever any family member would show up near Arnold, Mary would throw together a get- together. Again, these were filled with great memories. You all have your memories of these celebrations.

All of this to say, I, Doris, have that same gift of hospitality. Nothing energizes me more than to have a party at my house. I think my favorite is to do a "pot luck." But really any excuse will work for me to put the sign in the front yard: "Y'ALL COME."

My daughter, Janet has that same gift. It may have skipped a generation. But when Mia Stier was nine months old, her mom Michelle and her dad Kevin had the opportunity to attend the Marine Corp Ball, they asked Janet and Doris to go to Washington D.C. and take care of Mia for the week end. We had not really had

The Shaws Multiplied

the care of a baby for many years. We knew it would be fun as well as funny. We even thought it would be a good message for a movie called "Two Grammies and a Baby." But as it turned out Mia entertained us!!! Guess that hospitality gift has been passed down to Mia, the youngest member of this family. Such memories.

"Be joyful in hope, patient in affliction, faithful in prayer."
Romans 12:12.

GOD TURNED BEAUTY FROM ASHES BY MARY FRANCES (SHAW) HUNSE

These modern mothers who have painless births, with the help of Epidurals, have nothing on my mother who gave birth to ten children without a doctor. Back then it was unusual for newborns to survive. She birthed ten successfully. I being the eighth child arrived November 10, 1907. They tell me I only weighed four pounds and that my daddy put me in his shoebox just to see if I would fit. (He wore a size 7 shoe.) I had big brown eyes and reddish brown hair. As a youngster I was always small and slender until after my high school days.

My brother, Clifford was eleven years older than I. He watched me a lot. He carried me from place to place taking pride in carrying me on his back with my feet in the hip pockets of his overalls leaving his hands free to do his feedings. One evening he sat me in the feed box while he went up in the hayloft to hay the horses. My brother, Joe, not knowing where I was let the horses in the barn. Clifford heard me cry out, "Dick! Don't you bite the baby!"

Transportation was not good in those days. We went everywhere in a "spring wagon" pulled by horses. Therefore most of us didn't go anywhere. We lived nine miles north of Callaway. My dad went to town about once a month for the few groceries we bought. I remember going along just once. There was a mare and her colt tied at the hitching post. I ran over to pet the colt and the mother kicked

The Shaws Multiplied

me. The man who owned the horses picked me up. Many people had gathered giving me pennies to keep me from crying.

Our school was three and a half miles from our home. Kindergarten did not exist. So at 7 years I joined my brothers and sister in the long walk for my first year of school. My aunt's sister, Blanche Roby, was my teacher. I got along fine even though I know I was pretty badly spoiled. By then I had a baby sister, Ruth, I still referred to myself as the baby as did the other members of my family.

During one Summer I had a siege of measles with such a high fever that every strand of my light reddish brown hair fell out. My new hair was real thick and a glossy black.

The next year in March my little brother, Franklin, was born. My father was a contractor and builder. Consequently he was away a lot. My mother tired easily. We had no conveniences in our home. Mother did not awaken as soon as we did that winter. My older sister, Marjorie, got breakfast and made lunches for school. One December day, my mother was not up when we were ready to go to school. We had no way of knowing what the temperature was. The air was still. Afterwards we learned that it was 22 degrees below zero. The older children kept asking me if I was cold. At first my hands were cold. But as we went on they seemed to warm up. When I got in sight of the school house I ran on ahead of the other kids but, I could not open the door. It was as if I had no fingers. So I kicked at the door. Miss Jensen came to the door to let me in. I went up to the front of the room by the fire. Miss Jensen pulled off my mittens and my fingers were frozen stiff and black. It was late by the time my brother came after me as we had no telephone. In the meantime I lay on the recitation bench with my hands in a basin of snow.

My grades had been quite good. The girl, Melinda, who was in my class, did not do as well as I. She was always jealous of my grades. Without thinking Melinda said, "Oh, goody. I'll get ahead of her now." Although I was only 8 years old, I decided then to be a teacher. I said, "A person can teach school without hands. What matters is that they have it in their head." As you know, I am a teacher and Melinda just barely made it through eighth grade.

Doris Howe

Well, I missed the remainder of that term. When the doctor who was called from Calloway said he would have to remove my hands or he wouldn't be responsible for my life. I can still hear my dad say, "Oh, no. Any old stump is better than none." So he called Dr. Robinson from Arnold fifteen miles away. By the last day of school two of my fingers were healed up enough to have them in fingerstalls.

Mrs. Jensen asked my brothers and sisters to bring me to the last day picnic. Of course, I went. Mrs. Jensen had me read my books. I worked the problems in my head. I did all right and Mrs. Jensen passed me to the third grade. My classmates did not approve of this, as I had not attended school. What else could I do without the use of hands? They did not know that my dad had made me a bench that fit over my lap. I laid my hands on it and studied continually. My older brothers turned the pages and helped me. My older sister fed me.

That last day of school, Melinda was there. She heard Mrs. Jensen have me read. She remarked, "Oh, well. She'll never be able to write.' As soon as my fingers healed enough for me to hold a pen, my dad bought ink by the quart and paper by the ream and I got to work. I earned certificates for writing achievements.

There were two families who lived a quarter of a mile from school. The teachers always boarded with one of these families. The teachers did just what their temporary home folks said. Both of these families made up the school board.

In my fifth year in school, we had a teacher from Omaha. She quit teaching in February, because she got so lonesome away from the city. She let us all take our books home to finish the year out. Getting another teacher was pretty impossible. The next term we all started in the next grade level. Nothing was said then, but when I got in the 8th grade, the school boards kids told our teacher, Miss Aydelotte, that I really shouldn't be in the 8th grade. Miss Aydelotte had to do what the school board said. Consequently, she took all of my 8th grade books away from me and gave me 7th grade books. They really gave me a rough time. Someone had a record "Lazy Mary" which these kids delighted in pointing at me while it was being played every morning.

The Shaws Multiplied

One night after dark Margie and I got on horses and rode the three and a half miles up to the schoolhouse. By the light of the moon we got my 8th grade books. These were the ones that had been taken from me. I studied 7th grade at school during the day and 8th grade at home by kerosene light at night. I passed the 8thgrade examinations given by the County Superintendent the first time I took them. Most students took these tests twice to pass them. After Miss Aydelotte found I passed, she started helping me. We worked problems on the board by the moonlight often staying that late. Miss Aydelotte would then attempt to walk me home. Margie would meet me on horseback. Then we would take Miss Aydelotte back home.

I worked for my board and room through high school. I was able to go home only for Thanksgiving and Christmas vacations.

My brother Jessie was two years old than I. He saw that I got to shows and country-dances. He played the violin and I played the organ for many of these dances.

My high school was four years of Normal Training in preparation for a teaching career. High School was mild in comparison to my grade school experiences—maybe even boring. I graduated when I was 18. I then taught for three years before marrying a wonderful man. We have three beautiful daughters and eleven grandchildren.

Valetta Frances Hunse by Mary (Shaw) Hunse
August came with its scorching sun
Gradating nearly everyone.
Women hunted for the shade
And served their men lemonade.
In truth nearly everyone was in distress
But one lady who was looking forward to—
With a child to be blessed.
She was the happiest of all the crew.
One night when the moon was soaring high,
Like a great eagle across the sky,
God sent the stork with a little lady
To be given this lady as her own baby.

Doris Howe

This child was tiny, but plump and sweet,
From the top of her head to her tiny feet.
She had lots of hair which was rich nut brown,
And she was as dear as any in town.
In pounds she weighed eight.
There was never a babe more tiny and straight.
The mother was tickled to death to have
The chance of all chances,
To hold her dear child close to her breast.
The next day, Babes old auntie, a dear from the west,
Christened the girlie,
"Valetta Frances".
Val for her daddy, the best in the land,
Etta for Henrietta, always lending a hand.
And Frances is the middle name of her mother,
Who likes the sand. (nix)
Now my little old kid In months only four
But she's hardly such a thing
As a babe any more.
She weighs fifteen pounds
Stripped to the hide
And I must say,
She is her mother's pride.

–Mary Hunse December 11, 1931

"Thou will show me the path of life: In thy presence is fullness
of joy; At thy right hand there are pleasures for evermore."
Psalm 16:11

MY "BEAUTY FROM ASHES" STORY—DORIS HOWE

I t is said that God works in mysterious ways. I had a friend in Klamath Falls, Oregon who used to say, "What will you be when you grow up?" At the time I was teaching in Hosanna Christian School—all subjects except science to 7th and 8th graders. I loved those kids. But I never felt a permanent resident in Oregon.

I met the principle of the school early in my two-year experience teaching there. She and her husband had spent the previous summer working as Mission Builders at the Youth With A Mission Base in Kona, Hawaii. She talked about it constantly. As a Mission Builder one actually volunteered at the base for room and board. All you needed to do was to get there on your own. As Hosanna was a new, quite small Christian school, they were not in a position to pay salaries on a 9-month basis. They paid us on a 12-month basis. This meant that I would get the same salary during the summer that I got during the school year when I was actually there and teaching. This meant that I was free to do something adventurous during the summer. Long story short: I applied at the Kona base and worked there that summer. They introduce you to the mission's work and experiences of others while spending those months on the beautiful island of Hawaii.

It was a positive experience injecting me with the mission's spirit. When I returned to teach the next school year, I was walking and praying saying to God, "When I retire, I will do the Crossroads

Discipleship Training School." Maybe one of the first times I knew God was speaking to my spirit, 'cause I heard, "Why wait?"

I had excuses that I thought were reasons. But looking back I can see that God was very patiently preparing me for where he has me today. For over 16 years I have been a missionary to unplanned pregnancies in young unmarried women who might be open to counseling regarding adoption as an option for their baby.

This was not the first experience that God used to get me where I am today. But it was God's way of starting me forward toward His plan.

When we are going through deep trials and testings, we don't necessarily understand them or that life will ever be bright again. During a period of some short years, it seemed to me that everything was going wrong. Years later the women of our church asked me to talk at a women's gathering and tell the background in my life that prepared me for what I am now doing. Really, all they knew about me was that I was working with a ministry to young, unmarried, pregnant women. In preparation for that talk I found that God had indeed taken several trials during those hard times in my life to prepare me for the current position.

I had walked THROUGH, with God's help, the pain of grief. Our son, Joey, was hit and killed by a drunk driver. My dad died three days later—I am sure of a broken heart in his concern for me. Grief comes from any loss. There are several stages in the grieving process. Mostly it is painful. More recently God showed me that most folks do not know what to say to someone who is experiencing a loss and is in grief. There are books to read and lessons to be taught. But the best response I can give for someone in grief is: I can be a shoulder on which they can cry, ears to listen, and arms to hold.

These young women go through grief. Some of their losses are the dream of the life they always dreamed they would live. The pregnancy changed their future 180 degrees. When an adoption plan is made for their baby and followed through, they grieve intensely. They grieve the loss of that baby in their arms to love and nurture. The pain seems insurmountable. I have learned that there are two requirements for a young woman to go through placing her baby for adoption successfully. She must know that God is directing her through that plan and that she loves that baby more than life itself. She must get to the point where she knows that her love for her baby will put him/her in a better situation and place than she can give at this time in her life. She does so FOR the baby. Then, there is life after adoption. I understand GRIEF.

Other experiences during those hard years that God used to get me here are as follows:

I understand the rejection that these girls feel when they are rejected by their parents and probably the boy friend. I went into marriage with the knowing that it would last my lifetime. But after 30 years, I was rejected. I understand rejection.

I understand couples who want a child and are not getting pregnant. Finally they turn to adoption. We were in that state when we adopted Jeff. Raising each child requires a different approach. After the fact, I know that no matter the situation that brought children into our family, each child is an individual and needs an individual love and nurture.

Having a degree in speech therapy gave me experiences in case studies. In this work with adoptions, I enjoy doing home studies with the prospective adoptive couples.

In adoptions there are many opportunities to understand the legal ramifications of the choice. I am not a lawyer. In fact my husband was in Law School while we were a young married couple. Joe had a high IQ, and was a "night person" and still he would stay up pouring over the books most nights until 3 and 4 a.m., I did have a nightmare one time. In that nocturnal vision, I was petrified because I was a student in Law School. I KNEW that was not for me.

However some of it must have rubbed off by osmosis. In this ministry I see that from the past I did learn some valuable tidbits concerning the law and for what I do now. The courtrooms do not intimidate me. I am comfortable around lawyers and judges. The most fun I had a few years ago I will relate. I remember hearing a "rule" that law students learn in their very first week in class. It is "never ask a question in court that you do not know the answer to."

Doris Howe

We were in court for a parental rights termination. In this particular case, the "birth dad" had not been located prior to the hearing. The court had appointed an ad litem to represent the illusive "sperm donor." There was also an appointed lawyer to represent the baby. The counselor representing the baby did that forbidden thing. He asked a question for which he did not have the answer. He asked me where the baby was and how did we know the baby was in a good, safe place. It was my turn to take the floor in front of this lawyer, the judge, the court reporter, and all those folks in the courtroom awaiting their turn for their case. I got to tell all the details of how we qualify the prospective parents, the 2-day orientation, the home study, their criminal background checks, and their references, etc. etc. etc. I could see that lawyer's mind recalling that first week of law school and how he was biting his tongue for asking that question. I was laughing on the inside because I got to educate a bunch of people who were present that day not knowing they would learn about how adoptions are done so beautifully well through this ministry and so differently from the negative thoughts so many have even today concerning adoptions. *I had my day in court!*

God is good. He, indeed, turned the ashes in my life to beauty, as he used all the bad for good!!!

"If you don't ask, the answer is always 'no,'" Doris

RUTH SHAW VICKERS

The youngest Shaw daughter was Aunt Ruth. She married Uncle Cecil. Aunt Ruth was always so sweet and kind. Aunt Ruth had a strong work ethic, was honest, caring, loyal, and thought to be the prettiest of the Shaw girls. The first year Shirley and I, Ted, were married they came to visit us in Loomis, our first home. Shirley was teaching in that town. Later they visited us in Lexington with their motor home. They brought their poodles with them. Imogene, Deanie, is the first daughter of Aunt Ruth and Uncle Cecil. She grew up with an entrepreneur, ambitious father and a pretty, hard working, submissive mom. She was able to go away to Curtis Agricultural High School. From that graduation, she then was the first of the cousins to go immediately to the University of Nebraska at Lincoln. She graduated with honors and a degree in Home Economics. With that background and education she went on to a very satisfying and fulfilling career over her working years. While I, Ted, was in the Navy and home on leave I visited Uncle Cecil and Aunt Ruth. Uncle Cecil asked what I was going to do when I got out of the Navy. I answered that I didn't know, but I did plan to go to college. He suggested I think about something in the medical field. Maybe that is what started me on the career, dentistry, I did enter. (From Ted.)

Aunt Ruth and Uncle Cecil would stop in occasionally to visit us at our farm about 3 miles from Arnold, They lived in Hemingford, Nebraska in north/western Nebraska. It gets quite fidget in the winters in Nebraska. And washing bedding isn't necessarily done every time someone comes and stays over night. My mother often took a hot water bottle to bed with her at night. Heat did not reach the bedrooms in that house in the winter. Uncle Cecil and Aunt Ruth, as guests, got to sleep in my parents' bed during their over night visit. Uncle Cecil would never let any of us forget about the frozen bottle water he found in the bed. His version of it was, we had put it there to cool the bed so they would not want to "over stay" their welcome.

Imogene, Deanie, Vickers Olsen.

Deanie got her nickname early in life. Cousin, Valetta 10 months older than her cousin, could not say Imogene. She called the new baby Deanie. That name has stuck for most of the family members all these years. Deanie acquired the nickname "Vickey" when she was in high school. That name came naturally as a result of her last name being Vickers.

Deanie is one of the family members who has kept the closest contact with Doug and Mandy's farm place in Pine Canyon over the years. Whenever Deanie goes to Nebraska, she makes it a priority to stop in at the old homestead. She has kept up with the various folks who have lived there over the years by her visits. She knows their names, addresses, and phone numbers. Recently when Doris, Valetta, and Jeff attempted to find the old farm place, we had a real adventure. The directions we got from Detta were written many years ago. They were very sketchy and mentioned several landmarks which could have changed over the years. The directions had no road names or numbers and only estimated numbers of miles before the turn off. After three "false starts" on wrong roads, we tried one last road. It took us several miles through the most beautiful country with green hills, canyons, and an occasion windmill. We were enjoying the scenery, but were wondering if this was another wrong turn. Then suddenly on the left side of the road was a collection of buildings—a home, a barn, a garage, and a windmill. We recognized the place because the barn had not changed over these many years. We had all seen pictures of that barn taken years ago. Today the windmill had a cedar tree that grew up on its own and had grown all the way up to the blades. This made the windmill seem shorter than we remembered it to be from when we had last seen it as kids. The house remained structurally sound with a few outward changes. This is a tribute to the quality of construction our talented Grampa used when building homes.

We took several pictures and were very excited to finally find the farm and recognize it. After we calmed down from the excitement and were back on the road in front of the property, there on the corner was a road sign. It read, "Road 419" one way, and "Pine Canyon Road" the other way." This also excited us because all we remembered is our grandparents lived in Pine Canyon. That Pine Canyon Road dead-ended there at road 419 right out front of the farm property. I said, "We've got to take that road. Maybe it will take us to the Pine Canyon School, where Mother went when she froze her hands, and the two of us attended for a few months when we were kids." So, we drove the road. It ended at Nebraska 92—the road between Arnold and Merna. And was labeled "Pine Canyon Road." What an easy way to locate the Shaw farm!! So, when you are in Central Nebraska and want to see the old homestead, you now have easy directions! However, you will miss all that beautiful country we got to enjoy on Road 419.

Imogene Vickers Olsen, June 30, 2013

In the last 20 years, I have often driven to Pine Canyon, Nebraska, the area where our grandparents built and lived. On that first trip, I stopped in Callaway and ask directions from a woman in a coffee shop. She told me how to find Pine Canyon Road. Back then no signs helped one find the areas. I recall she said, "Go toward Arnold on the Callaway to Arnold Road. When you see many large granaries on your left (about 10 miles out of town), take the next (sharp) right turn onto "Pine Canyon Road". That road is no longer called by that name. Now has a number posted on it. Continue on. As you drive along that road, you will see the hump back hills. The road is gravel and narrow, but you probably won't meet other cars that you need to give space. In approximately 3 miles you will see the Shaw home on the left. The home sits to the back of the lot." Sure enough, she was right.

Grandpa Shaw built the home in Pine Canyon about 1918. The family lived on Cliff Table area until the home was built. His son, Joe, helped with the carpentry work. Joe died in 1923 at the family home.

The first time I found the home, it was a thrill. The memories flooded back. Many things look familiar. The farm home still had the open porch to the south with steps down to the ground.

Originally the road to the home was from the south over a generally dry creek. As a young child I remember my dad, Cecil Vickers, helping Grandpa repair the planks over the creek to make it safer. That south entrance came past the windmill and up toward the house.

I remember the drives from Hemingford to Pine Canyon to visit Grandpa and Grandma. It was a long road. Highway 2 had many twists and turns. At Anselmo we would drive south on a dirt road to the Merna to Arnold Road. There was always conversation about the muddy descent into Pine Canyon down that steep road with washouts and curves on both sides. We would just hold our breaths until we got into the canyon. Then sometimes it wasn't much better.

Grandpa Shaw died in 1943. Grandma Amanda went to live with Aunt Margie. Grandma died in 1950. The home sat vacant for many years. One of the first buyers was, Mr. Swan. He was an actor in Western Movies. Valetta met a retired mail carrier from Callaway in Gothenburg. As they conversed, this mail carrier knew exactly the farm where Mr. Swan lived. "It's a small world."

Today's owners are Terry L. and Jeni Adams. They live and work in Berwyn and come to the farm most weekends.

The year Shirley Shaw Hayes came to the Shaw reunion, we drove out to Grandpa and Grandma's home. Mr. Adams was there. He took us for a tour inside the home. It looked much the same as I remembered it. They had built a bathroom off the living room and the back bedroom area by using some of the front porch space.

The Shaws Multiplied

The large pocket door from the dining room to the living room is still there and it works. This is another tribute to the quality of the builder, our Grampa Shaw. The kitchen had minimal changes.

What surprised me the most was as we walked up the steps there was a toilet right there! No doors or privacy. That was a shock. I think there were still 4 bedrooms. Shirley noticed there was marijuana growing in the chicken coop area. Probably a native Nebraskan would not have recognized the plant. This year, Mr. Adams said he is still cutting it out. In another area of the country this might have been a profitable commodity.

\Mom (Ruth Shaw Vickers) always wanted to go back to Pine Canyon. Once as I was leaving Hemingford to head back to Illinois, I took both Mom and Dad with me to Pine Canyon. We walked about pointing out things to help Mom's memory, but I do not know if Mom recognized anything or not. Hopefully she did recognize some of it.

When I visited the home this year, Mr. Adams was there. I visited with him briefly. They have added a new front area to the home and extended the roof over an area for a patio and chairs. We recall the original home being sort of a "barn red. It now has white siding. The dormer windows from the second floor give the tell tale sign that this is indeed the old Shaw home place.

The schoolhouse where Mom and many of her siblings attended, still stands. The boarded windows are not enough of a camouflage. It still looks like a school. It is on the right side of the road just before you go up out of the canyon.

The roads are now all labeled making it quite easy to find the old place in Pine Canyon. From Merna head toward Arnold. About 12 miles along that road, there is a road sign on the left "Pine Canyon Road". Turn left and follow that road staying on the canyon side of it. In a few miles you come to the road down to Pine Canyon. That road dead ends at the corner of the Shaw home and road 419.

"The Lord thy God, He it is that does go with you: he will not fail you, nor forsake you," Deuteronomy 31:6

The "baby" of the Shaw family was Frank or FD as some called him. He married Mable. Their daughter, Shirley, submitted the following:

My dad, what a story he could tell. I only know some of it, but I listened when he shared a part of his story. He was born on a farm in Nebraska. Sounds simple enough, but the man that grew up on that farm was as capable at building and fixing things as the brightest engineer, mechanic, carpenter or any number of professions that now require a trade school or college degree. He had abilities inherited from his dad—the delightful man we called "Grampa Shaw."

After a few years of "riding the rails" during the great depression of the 30s, dad finally settled down. In the early 40s, he found himself in Nevada working on a ranch. I believe this is where he met my mother, a beautiful woman who must have made him forget everything else important to him. They were married in Reno around the year 1944. After dad gained employment at one of the WWII era shipping yards in Alameda, California, they started a family. I arrived first on April 8, 1947, born in Torrance, California. Then, on September 14, 1948, my sister Linda was born. I remember very little of that time we lived in a trailer park. I do remember when we moved to what is now Citrus Heights, California. I loved the big Eucalyptus trees and there was a small grocery store across the street. Some of those trees are still there, although it is now a big parking lot for a group of retail stores. Later in life, I would find myself living in my own home across the street from that first family home.

I did not know it at the time, but the Southern Pacific Railroad had hired my dad. He transferred to the Roseville yard. Many men found great paying jobs with the railroad after the war. We pulled our trailer to a small town named Rocklin, California. The city was named for its rocky base of granite, some carried by horse-drawn wagon to the capital Sacramento to build the Capitol building.

Life could not have been better for my sister and me. My dad built a house on an acre of land, which backed up to the endless pastures of the Whitney Ranch. While building that house, my dad fell off the roof and broke his leg I believe. He did the work himself from the bottom to the top. If he had help, I do not remember. In 1952, the house was completed. I started kindergarten at Rocklin Elementary School. Although I loved kindergarten, my first grade teacher hit me once that I remember. Mom came to the school and made herself known. It made me hate school. Glad they do not do that anymore.

Although my sister and I adored our great outdoors, my mother was very unhappy. She did not want to be isolated in the country. Unable to drive, she would take us to Roseville on the Greyhound bus so she could enjoy "civilization". She got a job at the Roseville Tribune newspaper and wrote soft news. My mom loved to write. She even wrote novels. I do not know where all of the manuscripts went. Eventually it was not enough to keep her from feeling lonely, so my dad sold the house and we moved to Roseville for a while until dad found a house in Citrus Heights. That was not much better than Rocklin. It was not even a city at the time. The school was a couple of blocks from our house. Mom volunteered for the PTA. She liked to sew and write stories. Our home in Citrus Heights was not a happy one. My parents were not happy. Dad was working all of the time. Mom was very unhappy. This was the result of a 1950's housewife with the heart of a novelist, I suppose. She was never able to meet her professional goals.

I learned that lesson early on from my mom. Achieving goals do not come from watching soap operas and the neighbors. One thing I remember fondly was the Thanksgiving and Christmas dinners my mom made. My dad worked because the overtime was great. It was a big event when he finally came home from work and we had dinner together. Another fun time was when dad piled us into the car and we took day trips to the mountains close by. One time I stepped on a broken bottle at a place called Silver Lake. I still have the scar on the bottom of my foot. My parents had to run me to a local doctor. That trip was not much fun for them I imagine.

Visiting Aunt Mary and Uncle Val stand out as the highlight of my youth. I loved the farm and my laid-back Aunt and Uncle. I also loved visiting my mostly adult cousins. My sister and I had no relatives in California that we knew of. It was just the four of us depending on one another. I used to brag about my big family in Nebraska to my school friends.

In 1965, I graduated from San Juan High School in Citrus Heights, California. My sister followed in 1966. High school was a lot of fun for me. I learned to sing and act in the school plays. I was a soloist with the A Cappella and Madrigal choirs, which was not so easy because many of my fellow choir members had great voices. Our teacher once exclaimed after auditioning us:

"is there something in the water?"

Some of my classmates went on to form bands, perform on Broadway and two even became Miss California. So you can see I was running with the bulls! Mom and dad attended all of my concerts and plays. Linda also performed in plays. We had a great time. Well, until we met boys. What a mess! Everything went downhill; grades, ambition, the track meets!

My sister and I met two boys who were performing with the Roseville Civic Theater in a musical. After graduation from high school, my sister married her boyfriend, Bruce Cavins. Bruce's family was from old world stock. His grandmother would brag that they came to California from the East, around the horn by ship and not the cheap covered wagon route. My boyfriend broke up with me a year before heading to Viet Nam. Guess it was for the best since he came home with a severe case of Post Traumatic Stress Syndrome and was married several times before he died in 2009.

Forgetting my goals to become a Broadway star, I was married in 1965 to Kerry Keehn. His family was from Pennsylvania. He had a great family. In 1966, I gave birth to my beautiful daughter Joi-lyn. In 1967, I gave birth to a boy. He died three months later from SIDS. My first experience with reality I suppose. I was separated from Kerry and after the divorce, married Dan Hayes from Citrus Heights. Dan and I met in the fifth grade and dated in high school. We went our separate ways after high school, reuniting at a party. Dan had just joined the air force and was being sent to Korea. With a small child, I could not do very much outside the house. I attended a training class for clerical worker. Whatever happened to those goals? I always say that I would make a great example of what to do to mess up your life at a high school "enjoy your life first" motivational talk.

Dan and I were married for 23 years before we divorced. He continued to be my friend until he died in 2010. I still miss him very much. During our life together, we bought a house and had a baby girl we named Valerie Jean Hayes. I had to work to help out and was not able to be a stay at home mom as I had planned. While working for Pacific Telephone as a telephone operator and later a messenger, I went back to college and received a degree in General Science hoping to use it to teach environmental studies at our state parks.

The year I graduated, I signed up for the Animal Health Technology class at another college and graduated as animal nurse. I had begun volunteering for a wildlife care group in Sacramento and went wild over caring for orphaned and injured wildlife such as birds, raptors and mammals. I will always remember Dr. Barsaleau as the strictest teacher I ever encountered. He culled and culled our class until, out of the 50 selected, only 14 graduated.

I fell into my new title like a crocodile into the pond. Loved it! I was hired as the coordinator for the animal facilities at the Sacramento Science Center. This place had been magical to me when my parents took us to the state fair, which was the center's home at the time. During my reign, they were housed and still are, on several acres of land next to a creek with lots of old oak trees. This is the signature tree of the Sacramento Valley. I was able to take my daughters to work with me where they met many important local people who supported the museum. Congressman Matsui and all of the local reporters chatted with them. This worked for me because they helped give classes to visitors and did not mind cleaning cages. I loved not having to leave them with a babysitter.

As the manager, I had to be available 24/7. Few women had careers outside the home that were as demanding as this one back in the 70s and 80s. You can imagine the criticism I heard about my being at work all of the time when I had a husband and two children at home. But I could not imagine my life without this rewarding work. My work spread to home, where we had an acre in the new community of Citrus Heights. Finally considered a suburb of Sacramento and growing fast. Too fast. No place to ride my horse. Traffic had increased, but still no sidewalks to take a stroll safely. Dan built cages for the animals I cared for under license of the state and federal wildlife regulators. Most still do not know that they can be fined for keeping a wild animal without state and federal authority.

In 1981, our little house burned down and everything we owned with it. My mother died the day after Christmas, 1981. We were living with Dan's parents and trying to sort out our shattered lives. After work, I spent time with my dad who missed mom very much. I too, missed our long talks. It was two years before our new home was rebuilt.

Dad met Margie, whom he married a few years after they met. Everything seemed good again. Our new house was built. I had a new job managing the animal colony at the University of California, Davis. My career was moving up. I became a real professional and had just applied for an animal nursing position at the large animal clinic at the veterinary teaching hospital, when a horrible chain of events occurred.

Dan transferred to Visalia, California so he could move up with his company.

We sold our home and moved. Joi-lyn married Mike Idzinga and was about to make me a grandmother at 39! At first, we lived way out in the country for about a year, renting a mobile home. Finally, we bought a house in town. Valerie graduated from high school and Dan transferred again, this time to Phoenix, Arizona. This was 1991. Valerie moved in with Joi-lyn and Mike, staying in California. At graduation, she was only 17.

I had worked as a veterinary technician and as a laboratory technician at a winery, but certainly missed the opportunities I left behind in Sacramento. In Phoenix, I met the manager of Adobe Mountain Wildlife Center and once again found myself involved in a facility where 24/7 kept me busy. I was glad, because I was having withdrawals from having no children at home to take care of.

The Shaws Multiplied

My experience working for California Fish and Game helped a lot with my job at Adobe because I now found myself an employee of Arizona State Game and Fish. I was running a high profile center and became very adept at television, newspaper and even radio interviews. Actually, that experience began at the Sacramento Science Center. I loved it. I even had the opportunity to ride in a news helicopter to Page, Arizona where I released a rehabilitated eagle in front of the cameras. That was the worst part. You really did not know if they would fly or sit on the ground. This one went over a cliff and up she went! At Adobe, I cared for imprinted animals too. Like the young Siberian Tigers almost loved me to death. The young Mountain Lion had been part of a stripper's show. However she let the public get too close for photos. He bit someone! Meanwhile, Chelsie, Brittany Ann, and Michelle Idzinga had entered the picture. I had three grandchildren by the time I was 44! My sister Linda had three children, Orion, Ricky and Sarah, and one grandson. Currently she has six grandchildren and one great-grandchild.

When Dan and I finally separated in 1991, a few months after arriving in Phoenix, I decided to move on to a job where I could make more money. Who would have thought my lab experience and degrees would land me a job testing explosives; but it did. For almost 10 years to be exact. Valerie married Bobby Dilliner and gave birth to Kallista and Conner. She was such a good mother. Unfortunately, Bobby was not a good provider and Valerie eventually divorced him. Dan's parents took care of Val and the kids. She still did not want to move to hot, dry Phoenix where I had just bought a house. That was in 1998.

In 1997, I checked African Safari off my Bucket List. For two glorious weeks we traveled overland and one week we spent canoeing the great Zambezi River in Botswana and Zimbabwe. This was truly an eye-opening adventure. However, dad had been sick when I left. I was not going to go, but Linda said she would take care of dad. Still, I worried about him while in the bush where there was no communication of any kind until we returned to the states. Before I left for Africa, I spent his birthday with him. My sister gave him a birthday party where all his family helped him blow out the candles. The following year, 1999, my precious father died. I do not know how I got through it, but sang Shall We Gather at the River and the new Titanic Theme song made popular by Celine Dionne, at his gravesite. It was cloudy and looked like rain. Suddenly the sun appeared. At his funeral, a man who had been my dad's apprentice at the railroad shook our hands and told us what a wonderful person he was. When we described his life and skills to the pastor so he could read over his grave, the man looked up and said, "he must have grown up on a farm!" Yes, he did. They don't make many like him anymore. Dad loved his family more than anything. He sacrificed for us and I shall always remember him with love and respect. He loved his Nebraska family too. He was very sad when all of his brothers and sisters went before him. He loved hearing from his nieces and nephews. My sister took wonderful care of dad until the end.

When TRW folded, I found work as a program manager in the animal cruelty unit with the County Sheriff's Office. I was about to be laid off at TRW. This was the early 2000s and the roaring 90s with its deep pockets were gone leaving many of us reeling at the aspect of losing everything we worked so hard to get. Eventually, I did lose my house when the county program became too expensive to run. I found a job as a lab technician with an environmental testing company, but that too ended after six months. I was close to homeless. But my friend Heri, whom I met in 1992, was there helping me to get up when I fell. We are going on 21 years together now. Not married, but it seems not to matter to us. Love and friendship survive.

I guess the most tragedy I felt in my life was when in 2007, my daughter Valerie died suddenly of a heart attack. I had just gotten a job at U.S. Airways with its free flight benefits so I could fly more frequently to see Valerie and my two small grandchildren. Six months later, she was dead. The father had taken the children, using them to "get even" with his ex wife's family. Dan's parents, old and frail, would not play that game even though they had been a large part of the children's lives. They pretty much raised them to be honest. The tragedy continued as the children were placed in foster care; only the grandparents allowed to visit them because they had been in close contact with them and were considered essential. I was not! I had only been able to visit them a few times in 8 years due to on and off employment and trying desperately to save my home. Eventually, the children were given custody to Bobby's aunt and uncle. Seem like nice people. The kids are safe and that is all that matters. I had more access to them when Dan and his parents were alive. They are all dead now. The only time I was able to talk to and see my grandchildren was at these funerals. Those two little ones have seen far more death and tragedy than I did at their age. Too sad. Moving on... .

About three months after Valerie died, my family convinced me to take the trip to Hawaii that Val and I had planned. I was grieving pretty hard, but thought they might be right. So I flew to Honolulu and visited Pearl Harbor. This was the start of many trips to visit WWII memorials. Then I flew to The Big Island and rented a car. I pretty much drove around the big island from Kona to Hilo, crying my eyes out; bargaining with Him to bring her back; and seeing the wonders of our planet all at the same time. That wasn't so bad except I could not seem to get the pay phones to work and was afraid my family was worried I might drive off the edge of the volcano.

I had many conversations with Valerie during that week of driving in circles; literally, and joining her before my time was not one of them. You would think that a job where angry customers are the norm on a daily basis, would NOT be a good match for a grieving mother, but they took my mind off something that made their missed plane look pretty small. Not to them, of course, but I was very patient when others might have walked away from them. I was glad they were alive to yell at me.

I had my first vacation coming up. Three weeks and did not know what to do. Being a WWI and II history buff, I decided to visit Poland. Planning this trip was such great therapy for me. If I was not planning, I would sink into a deep depression. So I planned. I learned Polish. I read more about WWII and the death camps, of which I had studied since I was old enough to be interested in such things. My dad and I used to watch films of the camps on the old black and white television we had in the 50s. There was no censorship… that I remember. Finally the day of departure came. I found myself in the Chicago O'Hare boarding area with a whole lot of people speaking Polish. I had studied it so much that even if I did not understand every word, I felt comfortable with the dialect. An old Polish man sat next to me on the LOT flight to Krakow, Poland. Lots of WWII history there mostly pertaining to the Jewish people and their persecution by the Nazi regime. The old man did not seem to like my reason for visiting Poland. I cannot blame him. After two weeks in Krakow, I learned that Poland is much more than death camps. It is a great and ancient people who have learned to live with what God gives them. Some of the old Communists looked a little grim, but the youngsters were vibrant and a lot of fun to be around. The old man could not believe I was traveling alone. In fact, he was flabbergasted. Why not? I asked wondering if I missed a state department warning or something. So, when we landed, he would not let me take the bus to town alone. He walked with me all the way to the hostel and would not leave until he checked it out to see if it was suitable for me. After he left, the young woman manning the check-in counter asked if I knew him. No, not even his name, I told her. Funny story.

So I lived at Mama's Hostel in the middle of old town for a little over a week. I visited Kazimerz, the old Jewish neighborhood where I sat humbly in an old Synogue. I took a walking tour themed after the movie Schindler's List. We visited the ghetto, Schindler's factory and walked in their shoes. Alone, I visited the Wawel castle on the banks of the Wisla River, the salt mine and the big one… Auschwitz-Birkenau State museum in the little town of Oswiecim, the most infamous camp in Europe. I will never forget my visit there and my feelings as I climbed to the top of the famous guardhouse gate or "Death Gate", Prisoners might have seen as they approached Birkenau by train. This is the symbol of the camp; of ALL camps. I loved friendly Krakow where my meager airline employee starting wages went a long ways with the great exchange rate. I flew to Gdansk, where the first guns of WWII were heard. It had been German once, and they wanted it

53

The Shaws Multiplied

back. The Poles gave them a fight, which gave Hitler the excuse he needed to take the whole country away from them.

I arrived late and had a taxi take me to the hostel. Oh My! It looked authentically spooky. Big tan square two-story house nestled along the banks of the Wisla as it enters the bay and the Bering Sea. The cab driver was a brutish Russian guy who managed to get more money for the ride then he should have, but I was in no position to argue. I wanted to ask him to wait for me, but figured he would get all of my money if I did that. So I let him go cheat someone else and went inside. The inside was much cheerier than the outside. Think Psycho! The mistress of the house was warm and welcoming.

I put my things in the big dorm room where I found myself the only inhabitant. No worries about bunkmates keeping me awake all night. The next day, I got my tourist map and proceeded to visit the town. Amber, crystal and beautiful lace are the specialties. Poland's battle for freedom from Russian rule or "Solidarity" began here with the striking workers. Not too far from my room was a giant shell hole where a granary once stood, fenced in for safety. This town had been bombed.

That evening, I met the two gypsy men who were in another dorm. Glad I did not know they were staying there! I introduced myself to the owner of a shipping business who had a private room. As we sat in the living room chatting, he began telling me about his family. Then about his girlfriends, who had him to thank for all their houses. "Whoa, wait a minute. Didn't you say you were married?" "Oh yes, but my wife puts up with it because, in Rome she has everything". "By the way," he asked, "do you have a house?" "I most certainly do!" I said. Meanwhile, the two gypsy guys had cranked up some obviously gypsy music and were jumping up and down on the couch. I found this crazy dancing quite amusing. The mistress of the house did not and fell on them, using words I was better off not understanding.

The ship buyer turned out to be a nice gentleman and companion for my touring. He even took me to the maritime museum where he paid for a fishing boat he planned to put to work. We went to the airport together, where he paid for the cab. Half of what I paid! He was shocked. Like I said, the "I don't speak English" Russian pretty much had me where he wanted me. This was a great trip for my first adventure in Europe. That was 5 years ago.

Since my first trip to Poland, I have been to Europe many times. I have visited many other countries too, sometimes in the company of my workmates. In fact, I am high on the list of most traveled employees in my work group. In September I traveled to the WWI battlefields in Flanders, the Somme and Verdun in Belgium and France by train and came away with so much to be thankful for. And bless those long dead soldiers for making it so. I think my final words would be to thank my parents. They sincerely wanted my sister and me to be happy, productive adults. We certainly were not rich by any means, but we had everything we needed to be comfortable. Whenever life seems to be a bit much, I think of that determination to stay together and make it work for the benefit of Linda and me. I cannot let them down. My mother never saw me graduate from college. My dad never saw me make my first journey to Europe. But I always move on as though they are watching and can feel some pride in their accomplishment. They are the ones who made it possible for me to fly.

"You can always find your way back if you leave a trail of breadcrumbs." (A favorite saying of Doris.)

MARY AND VAL: (AGAIN)

I am the middle daughter born to Val and Mary (Shaw) Hunse. My parents were hard working farmers at heart. Because of an unfortunate circumstance in their lives when I was two years old, we as a family moved from Nebraska to Chicago. It was my parents' plan to both work, save their money, return to Nebraska, buy a farm, and settle in. After eleven years in the city, the hard work really became a "way of life."

Back to the farm:

We lived in the city of Chicago during World War II. I remember we had sugar and gas rationing. Being farmers at heart and the fact that we had an empty city lot next to the one on which our house and garage stood we planted a LARGE "Victory" garden. With that came the work ethic of gardening and all that entails—hoeing, weeding, harvesting, cleaning, canning, etc.

It was then in 1946 that my parents' dream came to reality and a farm was bought nearly 3 miles north east of Arnold, Nebraska. Life was hard. Farming is definitely not for sissies. It is a gamble all the way. The climate, the soil, the varmints, and the trouble with machinery breaking down all continued to build strength of character into Val and Mary. Money was short so Mary took teaching jobs in country schools—sometimes far enough away that she had to stay the week. Other times she had to battle extreme snow and mud in the country roads. But they persevered.

When we moved to the farm, gardening was again a big part of the grocery supply. I remember friends from Chicago came to visit us one summer. The wife piled her plate to overflowing with fresh, green, red, orange and yellow garden veggies, and home grown sizzling fried chicken and/or pork chops. With all that food on her plate, she was the last to finish eating. She commented that she always ate slowly. Another comment that we heard loudly and clearly was, "And this is all free!" We were thinking ("yea, right.")

Even with gas rationing, we were able to save the gas coupons and still be able to make the drive to Nebraska a few summers. Those were special trips that we often called vacations. I remember us teasing my mother about her keeping her suitcase packed. The reason behind her practice was in case someone was to take a trip, she would be ready to go along. That trait followed down to us girls. The stories of two vacations will be inserted later.

"Behold, I make all things new." Revelation 21:5

TECHNOLOGY'S ADVANCEMENT

Rriiinnnggg, Rrriiiinnnnggg. Ring. Two longs and a short. Did anyone hear the shrill ringing? That was OUR ring. Someone is calling us on the phone. Problem is that every other person on the rural country phone party line also heard the ring. It was like an announcement that someone wants to talk to a Hunse family member. It must be important because people didn't really use the phone much in those days. Yes, everyone on the party line knew a call was coming in. The talks were either an important newsworthy item, or just an interesting tidbit of information that could be turned into a juicy gossip subject. People were starved for something to liven up their "boring" lives. No TV's were in those country homes, yet. Entertainment in most homes was in the form of the really great radio programs that followed one another in the evenings, if electricity had come out that far into the country. So for entertainment, the party line was a sure thing—just the ticket! Today, we don't hear a code ring to tell us that a neighbor has an incoming call. But we do have "caller ID" which allows us to not answer if we don't want to talk to the caller. Makes it handy.

In today's society, people brag and announce that they have 3 or 400 personal "friends" on face book. As I understand it, this is the modern way of letting all these friends—and anyone else who could get into your face book—know every little detail of their lives. Just how personal are those friendships? And where did all this start?

Doris Howe

Was the old "Party line" phone service a "forerunner" of the modern face book?

When we moved to Nebraska, in 1946 we had a telephone party line. Today it would be call an antique. I just looked up the word "Party." It is a social gathering for pleasure or amusement or a group of people gathered together to participate in an activity. In the old rural telephone lines, these may have been one of the few things those folks did for amusement. No one had TV. And computer games had not even yet been invented. You see, each member on the line had a "code" ring. I think ours was two longs and a short. The interesting thing was that we, as well as everyone else on the line, heard the ring codes of all the others on the party line. It was sort of a signal that others could keep up dated on the affairs of the others on the party line, as they could listen in to the conversation. It was sort of like the now face book, but on a much smaller basis.

If we wanted to purposely talk with someone else on the line, we knew their ring code and could crank it, announcing to all the others that we had something to say to that friend. IF you wanted to call someone not on your party line, you cranked one long ring on the phone box. That got the operator's attention from her switchboard in town. Also, she would get the message first hand before anyone else—sort of a "fringe benefit" from her job as the telephone operator.

All of this seems very antiquated. I also remember an article in the National Geographic including pictures of the first computer. It was the size of a large city block.

Today, many folks have an instrument that fits in the palm of their hand. It is a phone, a computer to get and send emails, a method to "google" and find the answer to any pressing question, (maybe a modernized Encyclopedia Britatinacia), do business transactions, a GPS, a camera, to take pictures and movies and send and receive both, plus probably more things than I can even relate to. Folks can send coded messages, called texting, to anyone who may also have one of these modern conveniences. And get an instant reply. I have come into the 21st century kicking and screaming. My cell phone allows me to make and receive phone calls period. Having taught

English grammar for so many years, it goes against my grain to purposely misspell words and use poor grammar just to be IN. And I remember my son-in-law's remark as it fits me so well. "You get away from that wheel barrow. You know you don't know nothing about complicated machinery."

A few months ago I got this epistle. I think it fits here and will quote it for you: The author is unknown, but obviously a "senior citizen.'

"When I bought my Blackberry I thought about the 30-year business I ran with 1800 employees, all without a cell phone that plays music, takes videos, pictures and communicates with Facebook and Twitter. I signed up under dress for Twitter and Facebook, so my seven kids and their spouses, 13 grandkids and 2 great grand kids could communicate with me in the modern way. I figured I could handle something as simple as Twitter with only 140 characters of space.

"That was before one of my grandkids hooked me up for Tweeter, Tweetree, Twhirl, Twitterfon, Tweetie, and Twittererific Tweetdeck, Twitpix and something that sends every message to my cell phone and every other program within the texting world.

"My phone was beeping every three minutes with the details of everything except the bowel movements of the entire next generation. I am not ready to live like this. I keep my cell phone in the garage in my golf bag.

"The kids brought me a GPS for my last birthday because they say I get lost every now and then going over to the grocery store or library. I keep that in a box under my tool bench with the Blue tooth (it's red) phone I am supposed to use when I drive. I wore it once and was standing in line at Barns and Noble talking to my wife and everyone in the nearest 50 yards was glaring at me. I had to take my hearing aid out to use it, and I got a little loud.

"I mean the GPS looks pretty smart on my dash board, but the lady inside that gadget was the most annoying, rudest person I had run into in a long time. Every 10 minutes, she would sarcastically say, "Re-calc-ul-at-ing." You would think that she could be nicer., It was like she could barely tolerate me. She would let go with a deep sigh and then tell me to make a U-turn at the next light. Then if I made a right turn instead… well, it was not a good relationship.

"When I get really lost now, I call my wife and tell her the name of the cross streets and while she is starting to develop the same tone as Gypsy, the GPS lady, at least she loves me.

"To be perfectly frank, I am still trying to learn how to use the cordless phones in our house. We have had them for 4 years, but I still haven't figured out how I can lose three phones all at once and have to run around digging under chair cushions and checking bathrooms and the dirty laundry baskets when the phone rings.

"The world is just getting too complex for me. They even mess me up every time I go to the grocery store. You would think they could settle on something themselves but this sudden, "Paper or Plastic?" every time I check out it just knocks me for a loop. I bought some of those cloth reusable bags to avoid looking confused but I never remember to take them in with me.

"Now I toss it back to them. When they ask me, "Paper or Plastic?" I just say, "Doesn't matter to me, I am bi-sacksual." Then it's their turn to stare at me with a blank look.

"I was recently asked if I tweet. I answered, No, but I do toot a lot." If you are not over 50 you might not understand the situation I have found myself in." Author unknown.

Are you in the IN crowd? Do you have an I-Phone or something even more modern? Or are you longing for the "good old days" of the party line? I leave it up to you.

"After a total wipe out from a hail storm, the house plants are safe," And "On a hot July day, one can watch the corn grow." Val Hunse

When the hail stones were as big as baseballs, Uncle Ora said, "Gather the ice, get the freezer and lets make ice cream." (another indication of the positive attitude of these family members.)

FARMING WITH IRRIGATION

It was the hot summer of 1954 when Valetta, Doris, and Mary Kay were employed by Val Hunse (for their room and board). Their jobs included moving irrigation pipes across the cornfield. They had the routine down pat. As the corn grew taller, extensions were added to the pipes. This changed the routine some. But, no problem, they just used those extensions to lift the pipes above the tall corn as well as above their heads. The exercise was so good for them. Like they say, "The corn was as high as an elephant's eye." The pipes needed to be moved routinely every so often during the day.

As it happened one Sunday afternoon, cousin Detta and Ham came to visit Aunt Mary and Uncle Val. During that visit it became time to move the irrigation pipes. The girls were ready. Ham didn't want to be outdone by three young, skinny girls, so he offered to help. It being Sunday afternoon, Ham and Detta had come right from their church service. Ham needed help in preparing for the task ahead of them. They found some bibbed overalls, and pair of 4 buckle overshoes to dress him. Looking back every time Ham tells the story it gets a bit exaggerated. He says that the girls were "scantily dressed in their sun suits and were bare footed. Whereas he was weighted down with the attire they had found for him to wear.

EDITOR'S NOTE: The bare-footed thing is the way Ham remembers it. Valetta agrees and has said she can still feel that wet mud squishing between our toes as we carried those pipes.

When the three girls did the job, they moved two sections of the pipe at a time. They put the tallest of the three where the two sections met. That way the water remaining in the pipe would run out of the pipes making the pipes lighter in weight. The girls would walk quite briskly to the next spot to be watered.

Now with Ham helping that made four workers. The task was altered a bit. Now they could move three pipes at a time. Instead of the tallest girl in the middle, they put Ham at that position. They put the tallest girls on the open ends. This meant that the water did not pass out of the pipes, but gravitated to the center—Ham's position. Not only was he not familiar with their routine, he also was not to be out done by these three skinny, helpless girls. Additionally, in his attire, the overalls got heavier the wetter they got and the overshoes got heavier as they accumulated mud.

EDITOR'S NOTE: I don't remember that we girls started out to embarrass Ham, but looking back I guess we did. And as we all look back to that hot July day in the cornfield, we all laugh. From our point of view, we just were excited to have a man help us move the pipes, not "show him up". From his point of view, he thinks we maliciously "got him." But we all lived through it. In case anyone ever forgets the incident, Ham will tell it at the next reunion. Remember, he will exaggerate more with each telling.

Jeff tells his experience helping Grampa move pipes. He was in the field, with boots on, holding the pipe above his head. Grampa was called to the road as someone had a message for him. As Jeff stood there in the heavily watered field waiting for Grampa to join him again, he said he had heard that on a hot day in July one can watch the corn grow. Well, the corn seemed to be getting taller as he stood there. The reality was the corn was not growing. The weight of the pipes filled with water caused Jeff to sink into the mud. The mud was filling up his boots. When it was time to move the pipe to its new location, the boots did not move with Jeff. He stepped out of his mud filled boots. Picture the predicament. Holding pipes above ones head, bare footed, leaving the mud filled boots and unable to do anything but walk to the next location bare footed. Maybe later the boots could be retrieved. Maybe not.

The Shaws Multiplied

"If you seek wisdom as silver and search for that wisdom as for hidden treasures; then you will understand the fear of the Lord, and find the knowledge of God." Proverbs 2:4-5

LEARNED FROM GREAT, GREAT GRAMPA HARVEY YEAMAN

Other lessons my two sisters and I learned from my mother concerned the importance of education follow. All during our high school and part of our college years, my mother worked on getting her Bachelor of Education degree. She was constantly taking a correspondence course, writing reams of pages and getting a "C." She would take an off campus course for three hours of credit. She would go to Kearney during the "post session" and accumulate 3 more hours. This went on for many years. I don't remember exactly how many years it took her, but she did finally achieve that goal of a college degree, just a year before her death.

What this all said to me is, "I am not going to do it that way." I got my B.A. in three years and three summers straight through with no breaks. With that degree I had a major in speech and drama with a minor in English. Five years later I acquired an M.A. in Speech Therapy.

Most of my teaching experiences, over a period of more than 12 years were in English on the Jr. High School level. I came to love kids that age!! However I did teach in two different rural schools prior to getting the BA. Degree. It was back then that one could take "teacher training" in high school. I have to say that with that course in high school along with my years of experience, I learned more about teaching than I did in all the "teacher preparation" courses in college.

The Shaws Multiplied

Mary was an excellent teacher and put some of those skills to work with us girls. I remember when we were in high school. Remember money was short. My mother sat us down at the kitchen table one afternoon. She had a one- dollar bill in her hand and the box of kitchen matches in the other hand. She said, "Now that you are in high school some of your friends will begin to smoke. They will encourage you to join them in that activity." She then lit one of the matches and set the dollar on fire. We were astonished, but tongue-tied wanting to put the fire out. At that time, we could have got a ticket to the Arnold theatre to see a movie for 10 cents. No one said anything as we watched, wide eyed, that dollar burn all the way to the end. Then my mother said, "When you have money to burn, you can start smoking." Needless to say, none of the three of us smoked in our lifetime.

Another teaching experience during those years got our attention. My mother set us down at the kitchen table, our school desk. She had a water glass and a half pint of Jim Bean. (The brothers-in-law often kept one around for a "snort" if one of the others came by for a chat.) Again, my mother said, "Now that you are in high school some of your friends will start to drink alcohol. You need to know what that feels like." She poured a couple of ounces of the Jim Bean in the water glass and had each of us girls take a gulp of it. Naturally, it burned all the way down as it splashed into our empty stomachs. To my recollection, none of us girls ever became big drinkers. I, for one, never had a taste for anything alcoholic. I think my mother's "object lesson" and two other experiences in my life cured me of ever thinking "a drink will make one happy." Wrong.

When our son was almost 21 years old, he was riding a bicycle home from work in Southern California, and was hit and killed by a drunk driver. The story, as we heard it, is the driver had been drinking for 12 hours at the time of the impact. Too, our son-in-law, Joe Mike, came from an alcoholic family. The pain and heart ache that that family met throughout their lives was a vivid enough picture that would deter most from drinking (just for fun) or any other reason.

My dad was a tease with a gigantic sense of humor. His loyalty to his family was intense. He was definitely a disciplinarian. We didn't get by with anything. When we were in high school and living on the farm, we were allowed out at night only for a school function. "Play practice" was in that category. I was in every play I qualified for that the school put on. If there was a sports event, like a basket ball game, we could go, but our dad took us. Then, we thought nothing about it. That is just the way it was. We weren't allowed to go on "hay rides." "Those hay wagons are unstable and could turn over hurting and even killing some of the kids who were riding on it." (Smart dad.) He was also a "kid magnet"—sort of a cowboy Pied Piper. Jeff said he remembers Grampa Val's magnetism coming from his ability to talk to each kid as if he were a real person. He never felt "talked down to."

Jeff remembers a time when he was five years old visiting on the farm with his grand parents. He felt big, and important because he was to go to the hen house and collect the eggs. On his way back to the house, carrying the load of eggs, he tripped or stubbed his toe, and fell. The eggs were ready for the scrambling skillet, needless to say. When Grampa saw the whole thing, he said, "Your shoes are just too small. Common, we're going to get you some that fit better." So, he took Jeff into town and got him a new pair of Cowboy boots. Jeff still remembers that they were brown. There was no condemnation, just an explanation of the cause of the accident. Somehow that pretty much sums up the character of Grampa Val to a young grandson.

"I can do all things through Christ who strengthens me." Philippians 4:13

"What goes around, comes around."

MEMORIES FROM JANET

The best part of the memories was the big family gatherings. There was always plenty of fried chicken and deviled eggs. Later we all found that the fried chicken came from live chickens earlier in the day. It was okay. We did not have a friendly relationship with those chickens.

There was always coffee in the mornings with real thick cream and sugar cubes.

I loved spending time with Gramma Mary and Grampa Val. There were always lots of laughter and lots of teasing along with lots to do. I would help Gramma Mary gather eggs. I always thought the chickens would lay their eggs in the hen house. No. Those chickens would leave eggs all over the place. It was fun to explore all over the farmhouse area looking for eggs. It was sort of like Easter and the eggs hunts only these eggs were not colored or boiled.

On one visit I must have been exploring a little too much in the weeds. I came inside later in the day itching like crazy. Gramma Mary told me that I had chiggers. The next thing was Gramma bringing out the fingernail polish. At a time like this, who wanted to polish nails? But the nail polish was to cover the bites to suffocate the chigger bugs. It was gross picturing those tiny bugs under my skin.

Another part of exploring the farm meant to go check on the cows. I loved that. Checking on the cows meant saddling up the horses. Grampa would have me ride a gentle brown quarter horse named Penny. He would ride a hot horse named KING. We were out checking the cows one time and all of a sudden KING got really excited. Grampa told me to take Penny and move over yonder. There was a rattlesnake that we had disturbed. Grampa took out his pistol and shot that snake from the back of his horse! I knew that my grampa was a cowboy and my hero! To this day, my all time favorite thing to do is to spend time with my horse. I love to ride him. Even cleaning his hooves, his stall, and brushing him down are tasks that don't seem like tasks, but fulfilling activities. Grampa cut the rattle off the carcass of that snake.

When we got back to the farm, he put that rattle in a box with several other rattles.

Kids could feel grampa's heart of putty even though he wanted to display himself as a grouch. I think he had more "adopted" grand children than most men his age.

Grampa and Gramma had another farm "over west." Gramma Mary and I were to go check on the cows over there, but we had to drive as it was too far to ride horses. Gramma would speed up the hills, turn off the engine, and coast down the hills. She said it saved gas. It was a riot!! Better than any ride at an amusement park.

I loved traveling anywhere with either of them because the car or truck was big and fast. Grampa taught me how to drive the pick up with the stick shift on the floor. That was a lot of fun. It prepared me for one of my first cars, a Volkswagen Beetle with "4 in the floor."

They had a collie dog that looked exactly like Lassie and her name was Moffat. Grampa called her FIDO. But then he called every dog FIDO. This dog was so smart. She always knew the difference between taking the car or pick up to town as opposed to checking on the cows.

Actually Grampa had a special name for each of his eleven grand children. Each knew his Gramps's name for him, but no one else was allowed to use those special names. They belonged to our Grampa. I remember mine being "Scrub." He had a big draft type white albino horse that was raised from a colt. His name was Squirt. But Grampa called him Whistle Britches. Squirt loved Grampa. Grampa would take his cigarette ashes and drop them on the inside of Squirt's nose.

The Shaws Multiplied

Squirt would throw his head up and grin. Horses are sometimes like people.

There was an old stone house way out in the back pasture of Grampa's farm. Often times we could find Squirt in that house, so we called it Squirt's house. All of us grandkids carved our names and dates in the house several times and on several places over the years.

We were headed to town one day to get the mail. Another memory I had was when I was riding in the pickup with both grampa and gramma. I was on the passenger side by the window. Gramma Mary was seated in the middle. All of a sudden Grampa stopped the truck, pulled out his rifle, leaned across us two gals, and accurately shot the pheasant in the head. The pheasant was not a "sitting duck" posing for a camera shot. It was running along the ditch.

Gramma Mary was screaming and clutching her chest. I didn't know what all the fuss was about until later. The shell off the bullet had ejected and fallen down the neck of her dress! But, the great thing was the pheasant dinner later that day. I learned that pheasant was to be served "under glass." We had it served under plastic. Everyone laughed.

Gramma Mary's fingers were distorted and stubbed. My mother told me that Gramma's hands got so cold one winter, they froze. That is what caused them to look that way. Having her fingers unusual did not stop her from doing everything. She would brush my hair 100 strokes every night. She said that the brushing would make my hair grow longer and thicker. Guess it worked. My hair is very thick. My mother remembered her mom's "rule" about brushing hair to make it grow long and thick. So when I was born, I had a small amount of thin auburn hair. My mother brushed my baby hair. All that I had came out in the brush. I was balled as a Q-ball for at least a year and a half. This was before the invention of headbands for babies. My parents said they would Scotch tape a ribbon to my head so folks would know I was not a boy.

Gramma was a hard working lady. She died in her mid 60's. The family said that she worked herself to death. I thought that was admirable!!

Doris Howe

Whenever we visited, Grampa would make sure we got a new pair of cowboy boots or moccasins.

I loved spending time on the farm. I loved the smells and the way of life. I admired the victories as well as the hardships. All of these experiences have made me into the person I am. I love my horse. I love every part of that life including the smells, the brushing the horse, the cleaning his hooves as well as his stall. One visit we got to see brand new kittens be born. Another visit was filled with cattle alive and dead. Some had frozen to death out in the pasture. Some had over eaten corn and were bloated. Another time involved us grandkids finding a nest of baby rattlers. My Gramma Mary scolded us with such fury that I have never ever forgot how much I hate snakes—rattlers or otherwise.

"My grace is sufficient for you, for my power is made perfect in weakness." 2 Corinthians 12:9 NIV.

TERRY COLWELL

How does one even begin to narrow down a lifetime of memories into a handful of stories? I wonder if that is even possible. Memories fade. Past events merge with present day realities. Details change. Ironically, it's not so much the stories we share, but rather the meaning we give to those memories. The meaning is that which transcends time and space, and ultimately gives rise to our personal transformation. In the telling, we are able to discover who we are as individuals, as people, as family.

As I look back and re-rehearse my memories, I find myself surrounded by a love that allowed me to question my world and find my way. Some stories quickly come to mind.

The first ones that come to mind come as questions. Who actually shot Grandma in the butt with the BB gun that day? How many times did I jump out of the truck when Grandpa slowed down? Others come as an existential statement of identity. "I do say so, I am a Hillbilly!" Others dealt with physics. Two cousins standing outside facing together the biggest question possible: who can pee the highest? To avoid further embarrassment, I confess that I lost.

And there are stories surrounding the laws of inertia. When the clutch is engaged, the tractor will roll down the hill. A slightly turned key united a Buick with a barbed-wire fence. When a horse decides to give chase, running away is the best thing to do. And I can't forget the broken eggs lesson. Using eggs as missiles launched at the chickens was not the best thing to do. Grandma quickly made her point as she used my behind as a bongo drum.

To narrow in, to focus on a single event, I quickly discover that, it's not so much a single childhood memory, but a collection of events. These events created an identity as a grandchild growing up on a farm but also as a child of God, As John Wesley put it, "going to perfection in this life".

That one event, that collection of memories, all seem to center around one family ritual: the seating arrangement during holiday meals. Grown ups sat at the big table in the dining room. The kids sat at the card tables in the kitchen. And then, we feasted.

After the feasting came another ritual. One by one the kids would try to sneak into the dining room and sit at the big table. Sometimes we were chased out. Other times we got away with it. But, sitting at the big table was never our true goal. There was one chair that held a very special place: Grandpa's chair. To sit in his chair meant more than words can describe. To sit in his chair somehow made the world all right. There was nothing to fear, because in his chair nothing could hurt us. In his chair we faced the confines of our human weakness and invulnerability. In Grandpa's chair, we discovered hope for our lives.

And then, life goes on. In the living we make choices. Quickly we learn that the choices we made come with consequences. They can easily lead us down a path far from family meals, away from the table, and more frighteningly, far away from Grandpa's chair.

A lifetime ago I found out how true that is. It was just supposed to be a routine stop. I planned to get a bag of weed, then go home. How quickly plans change. After the usual sampling of the merchandise, something was different. Something was totally wrong. Some type of hallucinogenic drug was laced it the marijuana.

I made a quick exit. Before making it to the driveway, the full effect kicked in. I was losing touch with reality. And I was scared. With raw determination, I managed to climb into the safety of my car. I couldn't get the key into the ignition. Reality had abandoned me. I was lost, and I knew it. I was over my head. I was all alone.

Where were the good times? Where was the table. Oh my God, where was Grandpa's chair? They were nowhere to be found. Yet in my lostness, I found another chair. Upon it sat the God who created Heaven and Earth; the God who was greater than Grandpa. I climbed upon His lap. As I poured out my soul, I could feel His love wrapping around me.

Thus began the second phase toward answering God's call on my life. It began as a casual question during my early teen years. Who asked it isn't important. What was asked was. What if God wants you to be a preacher? Scary question, but it touched something within my deep subconscious. And almost instinctively came the reply: No thanks. Then came the running.

But as we all know, it is impossible to out run God. I tried my best. I did things that preachers weren't supposed to do. I was a guest in a handful of county jails. I was going to live my life my way. And I was doing it just fine until that night in the car. I realized that by calling out to God, I would have to accept His will.

It has been a challenge and a blessing. Some days were, "Good morning Lord." Other days it was, "Good Lord, it's morning." Standing helplessly with a family as death claims another victim; celebrating the birth or a new grandchild; living in the ebb and flow of life; it has all been a challenge, and a blessing.

Within the confines of human weakness and vulnerability, there comes a hopeful acceptance in our lives. That acceptance teaches that it is not up to us all by ourselves. It comes by the power of the One who died and is alive forever more. "My grace is sufficient for you, for my power is made perfect in weakness." 2 Corinthians 12:9 NIV. Terry Colwell

"When you pass through the waters, I will be with you; and through the rivers, they shall not overflow you." Isaiah 43:2

DORIS AND JANET'S VACATION

In August of 2010 Janet and I thought it was time for us to take a vacation together. She had a time-share in southern Texas near New Braunfels. She flew into Dallas, where I picked her up. After a couple of days we drove to the Time Share. It was great. Just a "stone's throw" from the condo, there were several canoe/raft rental places and some enticing restaurants. We had decided that it would be an adventure to float the near-by river toward the end of our weeks' stay. We really wanted our time to be restful with a wee bit of adventure.

The week before the trip, Janet had bought a pair on inexpensive canvas shoes in which to travel. She got serious blisters on her heels from the shoes. So the first few days we "rested" around the pool as those blisters healed. Starting our tans was a fringe benefit from the blisters, anyway.

I heard Janet say several times to folks we met, "My mom really wants to float the river." I had not mentioned it, but figured that she was the one who really wanted to float. Thursday morning began with the picture perfect day. The sun was shining, the blue sky contrasted with the gray/blue water, the various shades of green trees that bordered the river made a post card picture like the ones displayed at the nearby souvenir shops. Even the aromatic mixture of greens, flowers, and water rounded out the picture of a REAL vacation atmosphere. Our bodies had a start on the tan that would show folks that we, indeed, had a restful vacation.

It was the day to attack the adventure and the river. We made the arrangements to rent the raft and begin our adventure. I was not concerned with being on the river with just the two of us. We are not helpless women. Janet is an excellent swimmer. She started taking swimming lessons when she was one year old. Through her life, she passed "life guard" training, swam in synchronized swimming in high school, and taught swimming from our home pool during a summer break from college.

At the raft rental we turned in the keys to our car and waited for the worker to bring out a raft for us to begin our wild ride. We had our yellow and white Igloo with drinking water, sandwiches, fruit, and the cell phone. When the worker showed up with our rig, it was not a raft. It was a kayak. Still I was not worried. I was safe with Janet. After the fact, Janet said, she had some misgivings about two women alone on the kayak. She had dated a guy who loved the adventure in his kayak as it often turned over. She would never ride with him. Fade out. Fade in.

My inability to steer the rig with the paddle along with the kayak seemingly having a mind of its own began our first adventure. The first set of rocks we were unable to avoid caused the kayak to turn over on top of our heads. The rocks were big and quite slippery with slime. I could not get a good hold with my feet in order to push my head above water and to try to turn the kayak over and off our heads. In the process I heard a crack in my right knee.

We finally got it turned over and were able to hold on to it—sort of. But we could not board it again. As we hung on to the kayak, we floated about half a mile or more down stream and on the other side of the river from where we had been dumped. We lost the Igloo and Janet's glasses and the paddle (which I didn't know how to use anyway.) She is quite near sighted and could not see much beyond her hand in front of her face. She had not worn her contacts. Dark ruby red blood ran profusely from a 3 or 4-inch gash in the palm of her hand. Often she would wince in pain and say, "The guts are showing through the gash." I assured her that there are no "guts" in the palm of ones hand. Because the gash was so deep, she could see the tendons in her hand and equated that to guts. But there we were sort of clinging to a root of a tree down stream half a mile across the river from where we had been dumped and leaving a crimson stream of blood in the river.

Some happy, drinking folks came by on a raft and offered us a paddle. We took it, but still were basically stranded. It was at that time that I saw in the distance at the spot where we tipped over, something yellow bobbing in the water. I told Janet that I thought that our Igloo was there. She said, "Good grief. I will have to swim to get it, but I can't see that far."

I began to pray earnestly. And that Igloo made a b-line down that river right to us!!! She retrieved her cell phone. Because the gash in her hand was quite deep and bleeding so much, there was serious pain. She said she really needed to get to a doctor. On the land side of the river from where we were there was a small sandy beach like area. We managed to get there and attempted to call the rental folks and explain the accident. We had no paper work, nor a phone number. There were several possibilities and information connected her with one of them. She told them we needed to leave the kayak on that beach and get her to a doctor. The man was very rude saying, "You can't just leave my raft there on the river just because of a scratch on your hand." Janet said, "First of all, it is not a raft, it is a kayak. Secondly, this is not a scratch, it is a gash." The guy hung up on her. So we began our hike for help.

When we finally got to a road we could see the rental places across a huge field. We decided it was probably not a good idea to hike across that field because on the other side of the field was another row of trees. We thought that those trees could very well mean another river. Not a good sign. As adrenalin had obviously set in for both of us, we began walking down the road carrying the Igloo and leaving drops of blood on that country road. Eventually a woman driving a car pulled out of her drive way and asked us if we needed a ride.!! Hallelujah! Did we ever. She took us to the river rafting office where I retrieved the keys to our car. I told the guy briefly what had happened. I told him I could take him to the place where we had left the kayak. He said, 'No, no, we'll take care of it." Guess he didn't want a scene in front of all the folks standing in line to rent some river rig.

The next priority was to get Janet to a doctor. The folks at the condo directed us to an Urgent Care place. They wasted no time putting Janet in an examining room what with the blood dripping off her hand. There we were in our wet suits freezing, hungry and exhausted. Finally Janet said I should go back to the condo, change clothes and get something to eat. She'd call me when they had stitched her up. I did. It was nearly 1:30 by then. By 4:00 I had not heard from her so I called her. She said they must have forgot her because no one had shown up yet. She was out in the main area asking for someone to come help out. I went right over.

When she got someone's attention, they said, "Are you the one in labor?" If that had been the case, that baby would have long since been born.

By the time I got there, a doctor had finally come in and stitched up her hand. We were given a prescription for some pain medicine for her.

We spent the rest of our week lounging in and by the pool and reading. When I got back home, one of my friends said she almost called us, but then decided not to bother us as we were "resting." How true. The scar on Janet's hand is in the shape of a capital "J".

Now that we are experienced with river floating, kayaking and emergency visiting, call us. Maybe we can teach you some helpful insights for a "restful" vacation.

"The Lord will keep your going out and your coming in, from this time forth and for evermore." Psalm 11;8

ALOHA

SISTERS FIRST EVER VACATION ALONE TOGETHER, from Valetta's view point: (ghost writer, Doris)

For two years my sister, Doris, and I talked about taking a vacation together. When daughter, Kathy, heard of the prospect of such a trip, she said, "It needs to be a place that doesn't require a lot of walking. Mom tires easily." When son, Tommy, heard of the plans he said, "It needs to be a place that Doris is familiar with, as Mom gets lost in the McDonalds."

When Doris heard that remark, she laughed and decided that Tommy was exaggerating. So she mentioned it to me. I had to defend myself. So I answered just like any confident older woman would. "It was only once!" Doris will never forget that nor will she let me forget that. In fact, when we finally did take the trip, she worked very hard to always know where I was, just in case I was getting lost again.

We both wanted it to be an adventure and not just a drive round the country. We also wanted it to be restful and relaxing. Keeping in mind Tommy's suggestion that it be somewhere Doris knew, it seemed that all plans were pointing to Hawaii. Doris had been to Kona five other times through her association with Youth With A Mission.

At my bank a flyer was going around for a cruise and tour of the Hawaiian Islands. We looked it over and decided against that plan. First that plan flew us to one of the islands, Two or two and a half days were spent at that island. Then we were to return to the huge ocean liner and go to one of the other islands. This routine continued

The Shaws Multiplied

to all the islands. It seemed to us that there would not be a lot of rest and relaxation. It would be "go go go." It reminded us of, "If this is Tuesday, it must be Maui.' Plus this planned trip was hugely expensive.

It seemed that every week or so, another something would come up that was a potential "adventure." We just discussed it, laughed, and chalked it up to the whole picture of adventure.

So, more thought and conversations brought us to the thought that I have a nephew, Jimmy, who lives in Hawaii. He had often invited me to come visit and stay at his home. So, I called him. He was very excited to have Doris and me come. Okay, we could save money by staying with him. We even confirmed this idea with Jimmy right before we booked the flight to Kona, Hawaii. He agreed.

The next thing we heard from Jimmy was that we would need to rent a car because he was "at the other side of the island." Doris was having a hard time picturing where "the other side of the island" would be. Another step in the adventure!

Eventually Doris decided that he lived on the north side of the big island, the destination of our flight. We decided that was good news as we would rather find a place to stay close to the activities of Kona. Staying with Jimmy would mean that we would need to drive back and forth and sometimes at night the distance from the action all the way to the north side of the island. Doris had old connections in that area and she found a condo close to all the activities for just $75 a night. We booked that. It was great! We really wanted to be close to the action so we ruled out Jimmy's home. The condo had everything we needed. We could cook meals there, have two beds and two bathrooms, access to the pool, a washer and dryer right in the unit. Everything was perfect. We could not have got a hotel room for that price. So, we were excited. We would need to rent a car, but that was fine. We could take a day and drive up to see Jimmy.

Then just a day or two before our flight, Jimmy called me to say that he did not live on the Big Island. It would cost $250 each to fly to the island where he did live. So, all the folderol turned our to be "much ado about nothing." The adventure continued.

Doris Howe

I flew to Tyler a couple of days prior to our flight to Kona to be with Doris and sort of take the trip a little bit at a time. We flew from Tyler to Dallas to Los Angeles, and finally to Kona. With all the time differences and the hours of travel, we were exhausted. Systems time, we arrived something like 2 a.m. We had been up 22 hours.

We rented a car and began the drive from the airport to our condo. We were not given <u>any</u> instruction concerning the details of the rental car. Doris said she remembered the drive from the airport to be quite dark and unlighted, but she said she didn't remember it being THIS dark as we drove. It then occurred to her that she did not have the headlights on. Whew!.

We were sleepy, bleary eyed, and becoming "slap happy." By then, things were becoming funny. We soon got the "giggles" a situation that we remembered from childhood.

The agent at the car rental had given us instructions about getting to the condo. He didn't have very good handwriting. Lighting was poor. And the names of the landmarks as well as the unusual street names were not exactly what we needed to locate our destination. We ended driving several miles out of our way. We were on the right main road, but had driven out of civilization. Eventually, Doris turned around and headed back to town. We didn't know how to turn on the dome lights in the car. They probably wouldn't have helped much anyway. I tried to navigate from the hen scratches the car rental agent had written. They seemed like a language that was as close to Greek as I had ever seen. When I saw an occasional street sign, I could not pronounce it. This didn't help Doris in her effort to locate the condo. We had detailed instructions from the condo rental agent, but again we did not see any land mark that resembled our instructions. Finally Doris turned around and stopped under a streetlight in a tow away, no parking space and looked at the instructions along with the street signs that were posted.

We were right in the middle of another adventure. Doris could recognize the names of some of the landmarks and street signs that were foreign to me. So with that new information, we were able to drive to the condo. The next step in this adventure was to follow the

The Shaws Multiplied

directions to the parking space. By this time, we had become silly. Because Doris didn't know all the tricks of the car and she was having trouble fitting the car into the designated space saved for us, she had to back up a couple of times to get it right. Then when she wanted to open her door to be sure she was in the spot correctly, she could not open her door to look out at the parking lines without turning off the engine. This happened two or three times. Each time, she would need to restart the engine and try again. It was becoming so funny. Of course, you had to be there to get the humor of the situation. Finally we thought we were parked successfully. The next challenge in this adventure was to open the trunk and get our luggage out. By now we were laughing so hard we were weak and could hardly lift the cases out of the back of the car.

We did, though. We followed the directions to the front door of our unit. There was a lock box on the door. Our directions gave us a code that would open the lock box, which held the key to the unit. The instructions said, "Put in the code, pick up the key, open the front door, and you are ready to fall into bed." The adventure was moving right along.

Guess what! We tried the code for the lock box unsuccessfully time after time until our fingers felt like mashed potatoes. We did have a phone number for the manager that we were instructed to call ONLY IN AN EMERGENCY. Doris said, "This has just become an emergency." It was nearing 3 a.m. our time and we needed to get horizontal.

Even then it took at least another half hour before the man came to let us in. Naturally the first time he put in the code, the lock box opened. He wanted to show us around and visit. We could hardly show him any attention by then. But we were gracious.

Because of all the time difference we awakened fairly early the next morning. It was the next stage of this adventure.

During our stay, we did act like tourists on a vacation with adventure undertones. We found that we agreed on the things of interest we wanted to do. So, we did several things. We enjoyed going on one tour that took us to a coffee plantation. That was great because we had no idea what all went into making the great KONA coffee we had enjoyed previously. On that same tour we stopped at the painted church, which is still used for services regularly.

We did the submarine tour and saw all the sea life through the windows of the ship. We did a luau with Island Breeze entertainers and lots of great food. We went on a bus tour around the whole island in one day. We stopped at a candy and ice cream shop and the macadamia nut farm and shop. Most of the stops had Kona coffee tasting samples.

Each of the tour guides had tidbits of interesting historical as well as practical information to share. Probably one of the one that I will remember and wanted to be sure to share with anyone I run into who is traveling there is: "one can get the best view of a sunset from the elevated corner of the WalMart parking lot. Check it out.

We sampled 3 or 4 local restaurants and found wonderful tasting food. However, we did fix our own breakfasts every morning. Our condo had a deck above the pool where we ate the meals that we prepared. Probably the best bargains we were able to purchase came from the "market.' There we got as many as 12 "apple bananas" These are small, very ripe looking fruit. But they were the best tasting. Inside that black peel, was the sweetest, yunmmiest fruit we had not experienced until now. We got papayas, mangos, and acid free pineapple. All of these exotic fruits were for pennies at the market!! These special fruits were mostly new to me. Remember I live in the Midwestern U.S.

All the other times Doris had been in Kona, she did not have a car and just walked everywhere. She was amazed at the distances she had walked on other visits. We were glad to have the car cause we remembered Kathy saying, "It needs to be a place that does not require a lot of walking as mom tires easily." What she didn't realize is that I had been walking around my two block block at home at least once a day for two or three months to prepare for this vacation adventure.

Altogether, it was the most adventurous, restful, memorable vacation of a lifetime.

"Be anxious for nothing." Philippians 4:6

VALETTA'S MEMORIES

Valdemar Walter Hunse and Mary Frances Shaw got married January 2, 1930. They lived on Grandpa Hunse's ranch north of Anselmo when they were expecting me. They had no one living near. A while before I was to be born my mother went to aunt Margie (Mother's sister) and Uncle Henry's farm near where the town of Etna used to be. It was between Arnold and Gothenburg. My folks wrote letters as they missed each other. I was born August 11, 1931. Aunt Margie delivered me. Two weeks later Dr. Dunn came from Arnold to check on me to see if I was okay. He wrote up my birth certificate and wrote that I was born in Arnold.

Then we lived with my Dad's mother, Grandma Hunse, on one of their farms for a while. Just before my sister, Doris, was born, Dad got a job working on Ostegard's ranch near Etna. Aunt Margie delivered Doris. Her birth certificate says that she was born in Gothenburg. (We were born in the same house.)

Hard times found Dad without a job, so he hopped a freight train to Chicago, Illinois. Dad had aunts, uncles, cousins and his sister Gladys there. Mother had a brother, Clifford, and family there. When Dad finally found Aunt Gladys's house, he knocked on the door. Aunt Gladys opened the door. She took one look at Dad, who hadn't shaved and was probably full of soot, so Aunt Gladys slammed the door. (Probably she had several strangers coming and asking for handouts.) Before the door slammed Dad said, "Gladys," and she opened the door and gave Dad a big hug.

While Dad was looking for work and a place for us to live in Chicago, Mother, Doris and I stayed at Grandma and Grandpa Shaw's. I remember Grandpa putting me in a little red wagon and pulling me around in their house and laughing.

We moved to Chicago and lived in a basement apartment. Uncle Franklin (Mother's brother) came to see us. Uncle Franklin tossed me up and caught me many times. I could see the pipes in the ceiling. I was probably 3 years old.My sister Mary Kay was born in Chicago, Illinois when I was seven years old. My folks had Mammie and Kay as very good friends. Mammie's real name was Mary so Mary Kay was named after them and my mother.

We stayed with Aunt Ruth (Mother's Sister) and Uncle Cecil Vickers when I was in the second grade and Doris, my sister, was in the first grade. My cousin Imogene Vickers was in the second grade too. All our relatives call Imogene "Deanie" because I couldn't say Imogene when I was young. I remember that Uncle Cecil bought a new potato picker. Everyone was so excited about it being so modern and Uncle Cecil didn't have to hire Indians to pick the potatoes. Deanie, Doris, Dad and I got to ride in it. Evidently Dad was working for Uncle Cecil then.

We were still there for Christmas. We drew names at school and I got Deanie's name and she got mine. When we were opening presents around the Christmas tree at Aunt Ruth's and Uncle Cecil's, Uncle Cecil's boys, Jack and Dale, gave Dad a present. Dad could always guess correctly what was in his presents before he opened them. Jack and Dale's present to Dad looked like it was a winter jacket. Dad opened the present layer by layer and had a funny thing to say at each layer. Finally it was a man's tie.

After that we lived with Grandma and Grandpa Shaw again. Dad went back to Chicago to look for work. We went to Pine Canyon Rural School, the same school that mother attended. When Doris and I got our school work done the teacher asked us to plan a program to show the other students. We used nursery rhymes as our basis but changed them some.

The Shaws Multiplied

Grandpa Shaw liked to tease Doris and me and then he would laugh. One time Grandpa was asleep in his rocking chair and Doris and I put water on him. He woke with a start and wasn't laughing.

Grandpa used to walk out to the corn field almost every day to see how it was growing. He had a large rash on his legs from ankle to knee. He blamed it on the corn in the field. Grandpa had a long waist and short legs. It was hard for him to buy clothes that fit him. He had to cut off about a foot on his pant legs to fit him. This really upset him. We heard a lot of "dangs" from him. It was his usual slang word.

In the spring Grandma Shaw would make a nest of eggs in each of their small chicken coops and put a hen in there also. She would be so excited and happy when the eggs hatched. Grandma was a very proper and sweet lady. She never said an unkind word about anyone. I remember that they had a neighbor who was very lazy and didn't work. She would say," The poor dear must be sick."

A letter from Dad, dated July 7, 1938, told that he was staying with Uncle Clifford (Mother's brother) and Aunt Mary in Chicago.

When Dad found a job and a place to live, Mother drove Mary Kay, Doris and me to Chicago. Dad had many different jobs and we moved a lot. One time we moved into a house that was across the street from a Police Station. My folks remarked that if there was any trouble it would be good to have the police so close. Dad worked at night and Mother stayed up sewing dresses for Doris and me. One night a Molotov Cocktail was thrown through our front window. Thank goodness it wasn't lit. Mother was frightened and called Dad and the police. Dad got there before the police! Dad was working where the workers were on strike so that could be the reason we were targeted.

I was in third grade when we lived in Cicero, a suburb of Chicago. We were in an Italian neighborhood. Mother got a job working in a Defense Plant. It was WWII time. Mary Kay stayed with the lady down stairs. The lady never spoke English, always Italian. One time we were eating supper and Mary Kay said, "Taters, taters! Can't we ever have sketti?" meaning spaghetti.

When I was in the fifth or sixth grade Mother and Dad bought a house in Oak Lawn, IL. We were so proud that the house was ours. Mother invited Aunt Ray (Dad's rich aunt) and family to supper so they could see our house. We all cleaned every corner of the house. After they saw every room Dad's cousin Margaret said, "Your house is just like a summer home." Mother said, "Yes, but we live in it in the winter too."

Doris and I were busy baby sitting Mary Kay and picking strawberries and school. Our house was in a new development area. The school didn't have room for all the kids so we went half days and I went in the morning and Doris went in the afternoon.

When I was in the ninth grade there wasn't a high school in our district. I had to ride a bus to get to school. There were 400 freshmen and we had a building all to ourselves. At that time several local high schools were striking against having "niggers" in their school. We were told by some kids that at 10:00 a.m. on a certain day that every white pupil was to sit in class and not go to our next class. Before this, at noon some of the Negroes would teach us the latest dances. One time at lunch the principal showed up and tried to talk us out of "striking". My best friend and I were frightened, especially when she saw a Negro girl in study call leaning out her nails with a switch blade knife. In P.E. class we were playing volleyball. It was this strong, athletic Negro girl's turn to serve. She hit the ball so hard it just whistled as it went through the air and everyone hit the floor so they wouldn't be hit. My girlfriend said that her mother told her to get out of the school at 10:00 a.m. and take a bus home on the day of the strike. Well, at 10:00 am. Everyone went to his next class, but I didn't see my girlfriend. Quite a while later she came to class. She said that when she got to the outside door, a policeman was there and told her to go to class. That was the end of that, but the Negroes would give us dirty looks, friends no more.

Mother heard about an easy way to can food. Just put the jars of food to be canned in the oven instead of hot packing. We were all sitting at the kitchen table ready to eat a meal when it was time to take the jars out of the oven. Mother opened the oven door and the jars exploded. Mother was burned and cut badly. Dad was across the table in line of the oven. Dad was also burned and cut. He had a large piece of glass in his arm. The doctor decided not to remove it. It was too deep. He never did have it removed. There was glass, green beans and tomatoes stuck everywhere, even on the ceiling. I had gotten up from the table to get something from the refrigerator so the fridge shielded me. Doris and Mary Kay were not burned either.

Dad had a plan when he first went to Chicago. He planned for us to live there 10 years and then move back to Nebraska and buy a farm. We lived there 11 years and Dad bought a farm by Arnold, Nebraska. Dad moved to the farm in March. Mother talked to Doris' teacher and asked if it would be alright to take Doris out of school in March so she could go with Dad and cook and help him. It was fine with the teacher. She passed her to the ninth grade even though school wasn't out until the last of May. Mother, Mary Kay and I stayed in Oak Lawn until we sold our house. I guess there was a lot of talk in Arnold about where the rest of our family was.

When Mother, Mary Kay and I were back on the farm I got a job in the drug store. Most people came to town on Saturday and stayed late. The lady who ran the drug store had a soda fountain and my job was to wash dishes and they would teach me how to make sodas, malts, etc. I never was taught and I never could wash the dishes fast enough so they wouldn't run out of clean ones when they were so busy on Saturday. I hurried so that I cut my fingers two different times on broken glass. When school started I asked Dad if I could quit working there.

In Oak Lawn I had to really study hard to get As or Bs. I studied very hard four our first 6 weeks test just like I had to in Oak Lawn. I ended up getting all 100% on the tests. I was labeled smart and I didn't like that.

I was in a class that was very ornery and we had many teachers quit because of that. We finally got Miss Aydelotte, the same teacher my mother once had. Before she arrived we heard how strict and mean she was. We learned when she taught us; and the kids minded her. She was not mean but firm.

We girls were excited about living on a farm. It was hard work but the whole family worked together and we had a lot of fun. We had pet chickens, pigs, horses and calves. Dad, Uncle Ora (Mother's brother), Uncle Henry (Hank) would go hunting. They brought home a lot of pheasants. Dad was proud of being such a good shot and never would miss. One time he asked us to bring him his shotgun. It was about sun down. He saw an owl on the back of the truck, up on a hill by the barn, and he wanted to shoot it. It was quite a distance from the house. He became very upset because he didn't hit the owl. He kept trying. Finally he realized that it wasn't an owl. It was an old broom upside down in the truck bed.

The barn was up on a hill and Dad built a chute for the animals to use to get down the hill and into the truck when he wanted to sell them or move them. One time we were helping Dad load some big pigs. It was quite a job as they didn't want to go into the chute. We finally got them all in the chute. Well, the last one to get in the chute decided to turn around (in the chute). I don't know how she did it because the chute was very narrow. Out it came on the run and Dad was standing in front of the chute to stop the pig. Since my dad was very bow legged, Dad ended up riding the pig. Even Dad had to laugh about that.

We had a lot of friends from Chicago come to see us when we first moved to the farm. When Dad's friend Art and his wife came Dad woke them up by going outside by their bedroom window and shot his loud shotgun very early in the morning. It scared them but they did wake up. Dad thought it was very funny.

When Aunt Gladys's stepson, Harold, and his wife Vivian came from Chicago to see us our sows were having babies. They watched. It was really something for them to observe. They were really impressed at how hard we worked. Vivian told Doris and me that if we ever came to Chicago she would give us a job where she worked. The summer of 1950 Doris and I went to Chicago to stay with Aunt Gladys and Uncle Neil and cousins Dick and Tom. Harry went to our farm to learn to be a farmer.

The Shaws Multiplied

We were at Aunt Gladys's for a while and we still didn't get a job. It seemed that Vivian was a boss but there was a boss over her. Finally the big boss agreed to see us. We followed Vivian down in the basement of the store and around boxes, etc. When we finally came to the big boss, her eyes popped and mouth dropped open. She finally asked if we were the girls from the farm. We said yes. She said, "Oh, I thought you would be fat and we wouldn't be able to get around you at the lunch counter where you were going to work." We got the job.

My first teaching job was in a rural school near where Etna Store used to be. I taught there two years. It was the same school where my Dad went when he was in grade school. Next I taught one year in a school east and south of Arnold called Upper Finchville.

I decided to go to college so I could teach Home Economics. I took a heavy load of classes and went to summer school. I graduated in three years. I really enjoyed college. I liked the classes and made a lot of good friends.

I applied to several schools for a teaching job. The one school that I wasn't even aware that they needed a Home Ec. teacher looked me up and gave me a job in Gothenburg. It was really hard for me to believe that I could be so lucky. I always liked Gothenburg.

I knew Doris Williams Nelson and Ray Nelson when I lived in Arnold. They decided to have me meet Tom Delahunty. We were both invited to supper. Well, we liked each other. We met in March, got engaged in June and got married in August. We started our family right away.

Each class of girls that I taught gave me a baby shower when our first child was soon to be born. I couldn't get Tom to decide on a name for any of our children, but as soon as they were born he named them. I like his choices. Our first was Thomas (after Tom) Edward (after Tom's dad). Our second was Jerry (after a good friend of Tom's) Val (after my dad). Our daughter Kathleen (after a cousin of Tom's who was very pretty), Frances (after my mother Mary Frances, me Valetta Frances, and her dad, Thomas Francis.)

Doris Howe

I didn't teach again until our kids were in school. Then I substitute taught for kindergarten through twelfth grade. After subbing in a third to fifth grade room in a consolidated rural school they asked me to teach full time. I went back to college to get a degree in Elementary Education. I taught there five years. I went back to subbing again for one year. The Gothenburg principal asked me to teach elementary school full time. He gave me a choice of first, third or fifth grade. I decided that I would enjoy first grade more. I taught first grade for 17 years.

I have had ups and downs in my life but—my life has been a great adventure, <u>wonderful</u> parents, two sisters, relatives, husband with new relatives, children and their spouses, 7 grandchildren and a great grandson. Life is very great.

Valetta Frances Hunse Delahunty

"In Nebraska, it's how many cows to the acre? In Arizona, it's how many acres to the cow?" and "Kill a mosquito and all the relatives come to the funeral." Val Hunse

MARY KAY (HUNSE) COLWELL

As I began looking back over my years, I believe my life really started when I was eight years old. Nothing before that was worth remembering. I was all excited to be going to live on a farm in Nebraska. This meant going from city life in Chicago to rural Nebraska and becoming a farm girl.

We had the truck loaded with all of our belongings. Mom and Dad rode in the cab of the truck and my sister Valetta and I rode in the back of the truck with all our stuff. Our other sister, Doris, was already at the farm having gone with our dad in March so he could start the crops.

The many trees on the farm seemed to call me. It was all part of becoming that "Tom Boy" country girl. I found it exciting and an adventure to see just how many of the many trees I could climb. I would scout the lower limbs and see which limb I would use to begin the climb and eventually make my way as far up the tree as possible. We girls nailed boards up the main trunk to use for steps on one of the cotton wood trees. This was to make it easier to get to the lower limbs on the way up to the branches that were the goal. Valetta and Doris had me test these steps because I didn't weigh as much as they did. One of the boards came off the tree trunk as I put my weight on it. Naturally I fell. The board was actually nailed to my backside. They nervously laughed because they did not know just how badly I was hurt. It hurt. I don't remember our telling our parents. That was just one of our little secrets.

I learned to feed pigs, milk cows, bring in wood and corncobs to burn for winter heat. I loved doing all the chores. It was just part of farm life. I even helped my Dad when he worked on tractors for some of the neighbors. My job was to get the tools he needed. Somehow I would pick the right tool. My sisters had a harder time choosing the exact tool. I remember them saying they would go to the garage and stare at all the tools hoping the right one would suddenly present itself so she could take it to our dad and come across smart enough to pick the right tool.

Mom went off to teach in one rural school or another. She often had to stay with a family at the school all week as it was too far for her to travel each day. We saw her on only on weekends during those school years.

It seemed that soon Valetta and Doris left to go teach in a rural school or to attend college. I never envied them as the farm had become my life.

I remember a time when I was ten years old. I was sick. One of our neighbors stopped by. He asked me if he could get me anything. I told him I'd really like a white horse. When our mare had a baby colt, he was born an Albino, all white. I named him Squirt. That horse lived many years and became the favorite of the cousins.

A turning point in my life happened when I was 12. I was a pleasure riding Squirt in the pasture. When I was on Squirt, it seemed that I was always closer to the Lord. It was on this particular ride that I asked the Lord to be my Savior. To this day I feel closer to God and talk to him more personally when we meet outside. I often rode Squirt up over the table land to visit my friend who lived on the other side of it.

Our mare had another baby. I named her Beetlebomb. I confided in her a lot of my thoughts. Her brown eyes told me she was always on my side.

When I saw the Grand Canyon in Arizona, I was disappointed. I though the big canyon near our farm was better looking.

The Shaws Multiplied

At school I played basketball (horse) with one of the guys who was on the basketball team. I don't know if he let me win, but I beat him every time.

On a trip to Montana with mom and dad to visit one of mom's brothers, Uncle Jesse's family, I learned to skip a rock across a lake.

Fun times on Friday nights happened when the farmer neighbors got together to play cards. They would take turns hosting these times at the different neighbor's houses.

I left the farm after I graduated from high school. I found myself in Tucson, Arizona where sister Doris lived. I stayed at the YWCA. It was there that I met Harry. We were married and had 5 children.

Our oldest daughter Linda works at a high school in Colorado. Our oldest son, Terry, is a Pastor in Texas. Our youngest daughter works in a lab in Iowa. Our youngest son lives at home.

We have 3 grandchildren from our oldest child. We have 7 grandchildren from our second child. We have 3 grandchildren from our oldest son and 3 grandchildren from our youngest daughter plus 2 step grandchildren. We have 3 grandchildren-in-law, 2 step grandchildren-in-law and 12 great grandchildren.

When we were raising our oldest five-year-old grandchild we had another child. The two children were like siblings even though one was a really a niece.

A while back we sold the home farm. To me it was like selling 10 years of my life. I didn't want to sell it but I couldn't buy it so it sold. I got over the sadness because every time I would go see the farm before we sold it, something would be different. Things were missing as I remembered them. I would really feel bad. These were little things like the truck that brought us to the farm wasn't there any more. The pump by Squirt's house in the pasture was gone. Even the out-house was gone. Our Dad always called that his office. These are personal things that still mean a lot to me. (Mary Kay Colwell)

"Behold, I make all things new." Revelation 21:5

REDEMPTION FROM WATER FEAR

As I waited my turn in preparation for the very special event of baptism, I continued to pray for Jesus to help me and to give me His peace. But as I stepped down into the waters that flowed over me, I hyperventilated.

If the legend is true that babies naturally know how to swim at birth is true, I don't believe it. I do believe that babies do instinctively hold their breath under water for a few seconds. But swimming. If the aforementioned fable is true, it skipped me at some point.

I remember when we lived in the Chicago area: friends of my parents were going swimming on a hot summer day. They asked our parents if Valetta and I could go with them. The permission was granted. Neither of us knew ONE single thing about swimming and/ or water in which one might swim. The place of choice was a sand pit. Surprisingly neither Valetta nor I knew anything about sand pits either.

There was a definite stronghold of fear here that I thought originated from an incident in a sand pit years ago when I was in the third grade. It was there that my sister and I almost drowned.

I remember seeing our friends out a way from the shore. We assumed that they were standing on the bottom of the "pool." WRONG. But we agreed to walk out to there they "stood." Two or three, maybe four or five, steps toward our friends, the bottom fell out. I remember Valetta and me hanging on to one another and taking turns bobbing up on each others' shoulders. The thought that was going through my mind is, "If you go down three times, you drown." I was counting and watching the air bubbles ascending from my mouth, as was Valetta. As we were bobbing, we must have drifted toward our friends. At the same time, we learned that my long hair was golden in the sunlight even under the water. My hair is what our friends saw and came to rescue us. It wasn't as if I hadn't tried to over come the fear. That very summer of the sand pit incident, I began to take swimming lessons. My feet never got off the bottom of the pool no matter how determined my teachers and I were to help me overcome the fear. Keeping my feet on the bottom of the pool gave me a sense of security. I believed I was in control. We did learn to put our faces in the water. We even practiced the "taking a breath and blowing out the air in the wash tub full of water in our utility room." But that was as far as we progressed toward "water safety and water comfort" that summer.

I had always enjoyed sports of most sorts. When I got to college I planned to "minor" in Physical Education. So in college I'd taken a swimming class. Because I've always been graceful and a good mimic, I'd catch on to each stroke quickly, easily, and perfectly in the shallow end of the pool. I would even take my feet off the bottom. When I did the stroke perfectly in the shallow water, the teacher would send me to the deep end of the pool. EVERY time she'd have to pull me out as I panicked in water over my head. There, I was not in control. Finally I made an appointment with the P.E. instructor with my history and fear. She agreed to give me a "C" in swimming, but assured me that I could not minor in P.E. without swimming proficiency.

When I married and had children, I enrolled them in swimming lessons as early as a teacher would take them. It was my urgent desire that this fear was NOT going to be passed down to them.

During those years I again enrolled in adult swimming classes. I learned to tread water and I could do a sitting dive from the side of the pool.

Some years later when we had a swimming pool in our back yard in Phoenix, Arizona, I got to the point of swimming there. But somehow that pool seemed to be the only "safe" water for me. The technique was developed, but the fear remained.

It did become fairly easy to cover up that very real fear and continue to feel I was controlling it. I could go to a pool party while living in Arizona and socialize. I could go to the beaches when in Hawaii and bathe in the sun and read a good book and never go near the water. I even got to the place where I could "hang out" on the sport fishing yacht that my son-in-law skippered without noticeable panic.

But in actuality I only felt safe and in control in the water in my back yard pool if just one person who I really trusted was in the water with me. I wasn't even comfortable "swimming" with my family because it seemed to me that my teen-age boys were trying to drown each other or were "cannon balling" it into the pool causing what seemed to me "tidal waves."

So for years I lived this way believing I was totally in control. I was content with a bath and/or shower safely in my bathroom as my only enjoyable experiences "in the water."

Some years later I was attending a course in Introduction to Biblical Counseling with Youth With A Mission in Kona, Hawaii. During the Plumbline ministry, I casually mentioned that I'd had a fear of water as a result of almost drowning when I was in the third grade. I stated that I'd like to be delivered from that fear and I'd like to be able to enjoy snorkeling as well as the ocean beaches.

The counselors prayed for me. I prayed for someone to go swimming with me. I had learned to swim, but as I'd successfully avoided the sport because of that fear for so many years, it had become easier and easier to deny the fear and avoid the water and feel I had it under control.

God began to make very real the scripture that says, "God is able to do exceedingly abundantly above all that we can ask or imagine." Nancy, one of the staff women of the school, made herself available to me. Not only did she have a lot of experience ministering in prayer to people, but she had been a competitive swimmer and had also worked with reluctant adult swimmers.

The Shaws Multiplied

Nancy had access to a pool where she lived. She and I spent 6 or 7 sessions in her pool over the next couple of weeks. She was encouraged by my willingness to accept every challenge she put to me. And each challenge was a bit beyond what I'd have done on my own.

She kept telling me that we were going to snorkel soon. But first she wanted to help me pray through the fear to receive "inner healing."

During the time set aside for this ministry, Nancy prayed that God, by the Holy Spirit, would show me the root cause of the fear of water. I had always thought it was the sand pit incident when I was eight years old.

BUT. Picture the scenes with me.

The Holy Spirit took me back to when I was 2-years-old! We had moved from a farm in Nebraska where we had no indoor plumbing to the city of Chicago. There in the first old house where we lived, was a toilet with a tank situated high up on the wall. To flush it, one pulled a chain and water came swooshing down in, what seemed to me at age two, a GREAT TORRENT. The thought terrified me. Perhaps I could sense myself going down the drain with all that water.

Evidently I was abnormally fearful of that toilet. The ones I had used had no sound connected with them. They were outdoor or an indoor chamber pot. The day in question, as God brought it back to me, I had wet my pants rather than sit on the dreaded toilet. The picture God showed me was my dad ripping off those wet pants and setting me down on that fearful toilet with some force. As he did so, I folded like a jack knife and my little bottom touched the water causing me to be convinced that the toilet was truly something to be feared. I was sure I'd be "flushed" away forever.

As I described this "scene" to Nancy, she said, "Can you put Jesus in this picture?"

I did. There He was lifting me up to safety and holding me with love and concern and compassion on His face.

Because I didn't remember this scene until the Holy Spirit revealed it to me years later, I never held my dad responsible for the fear I had of water.

We continued in prayer. The Holy Spirit brought me to the scene with my sister when we almost drowned when I was in the 3rd grade. There were the two of us bobbing up and down on each other's shoulders and counting. We'd both heard that you only go down three times in the water before you drown.

As I put Jesus in this picture I saw Him reach out both of His arms around the two of us and lift us out of the water. Again He had that love and concern and compassion on His face. He then deposited us into the care of the two adults who'd taken us (two young non-swimmers) to a sand pit to play. As He turned us over to them, He reprimanded them for their negligence and irresponsibility.

The next prayer brought me into the college swimming class where I was pulled out every time I tried to swim in the deep water. However, in this scene I could see Jesus swimming right beside me cheering me on and telling me how proud He is of me.

As we continued to pray, the next scene was Jesus walking on the water a LONG way away from the disciples' boat. Peter called out to Jesus and began to walk on the water toward Him. As Peter began to sink, Jesus was immediately there to take Peter's hand. It was as though Jesus was saying to me, "I am with you, Doris, immediately, where ever you are—in or out of the water."

The next scene was the disciples in the boat during a storm. Jesus was sleeping in the front of the boat. They called to Him, "Master, don't you care that we will drown?" His answer to me was, "Doris, you will not drown. I have other plans for you!"

From this I graduated to snorkeling in a sheltered lagoon of salt water. From there I snorkeled at Children's Beach near Kona, Hawaii. My final triumph was to ride on a boogie board, the relatively small waves at Hapuna Beach. In giving away my control to God, I found that I'd gained a freedom. The freedom was fun! My simple prayer was really only a statement that I wanted to be able to enjoy the water as I was spending time on this island in the very middle of the Pacific Ocean.

No longer did I need to avoid the fun, think I was in control, and try to cover up a life-long fear. God gets the glory! My prayer was answered. God has not given us a spirit of fear, but He wants to take it away! He did it for me, and He wants to do so for all of His children. What fear do you need to give to Him? He is there lovingly helping us in every situation when we let Him.

"The Lord is my strength and song, and He has become by salvation.' Exodus 15:2

"I will sing unto the Lord, because he has dealt bountifully with me." Psalm 13:6

A PUT DOWN CAN HAVE LONG LASTING, NEGATIVE EFFECTS

From the information from Shirley Shaw and her interest in music as well as from Mary Hunse's high school days when she and Uncle Jesse went to dances where Jesse played the violin and Mary the organ, the interest in music and singing must have caught Doris unaware: Here is her story:

It isn't so much what we do for God as it is what He does in us as we attempt to do for Him." This is just one of the things where God has worked miracles in me. Maybe you can relate.

Let's go back to a time many years ago when I was a Freshman in high school. Because my sisters and I sang as we did our chores around the house, we knew all the words to all the popular songs of the day. So when we moved to a small town in Nebraska, I joined the Glee Club at school. It seemed that everyone did everything. It was only natural for me to join the singers. I HAD enjoyed singing, but had no real training. My voice is low and therefore I chose to place myself with the altos. Because I did not know how to read notes, I merely sang the melody in a lower key. Evidently this produced a "discord" to the director. He told me to "just mouth the words." As I was insecure in the new school and with new classmates, his remark broke my spirit.

For years I felt insecure when it came to singing. If the music director, who was an authority, didn't like my singing, I assumed that no one else did. My error. I was to find someone who did.

The Shaws Multiplied

However, when I came to other traumatic times in my life and I was brought into counseling to learn to forgive everyone who had hurt me, I was able to forgive all. In asking God to reveal to me everyone who I needed to forgive, the music director came to my mind (among others.) I did choose to forgive him. He obviously was doing the best he knew how.

But in the process of my forgiving, God began to do healing in me. I recall the first incident. I was in church during the singing. An older woman standing behind me was "croaking" out a joyful noise with all her heart. I felt that Jesus said to me, "I just love the way she sings to me." That was the beginning.

Next I found myself in Kona, Hawaii. Each Sunday evening all of us workers would get together, have some singing and a message from a missionary. This particular Sunday evening, the leaders could not locate the song sheets. They were at a loss. I said, "Can't we just sing, 'Lord we come into your presence with thanksgiving in our hearts to give you praise.' The leader said, "How does that go, Doris?" I ended up actually leading the singing that night. I had to laugh at the irony of it all.

From there I was teaching in a Christian School in Oregon. Every morning we would sing 2 or 3 old hymns to get us started. Once a month our class would all go to a nursing home and sing these old hymns to the people living in the home. The last time we went, I remember an elderly woman in a wheel chair sitting very close to the front of our group. I could tell that she was getting very blessed by our songs, The Old Rugged Cross, and I Come to the Garden. When we finished, she said, "I just love to hear you sing. Next time you come, would you sing a solo." Again I had to laugh at what God was doing.

When my outreach from the first training school in YWAM took my group and me to Ukraine, most of what we did initially was to go into the schools with our program. That program was to sing several songs and do pantomimes with the gospel message. There were times that I felt like one of the group of UP WITH PEOPLE singers that

Doris Howe

I'd heard years before. Today, I believe that was the anointing of the Lord that came over us as we sang to Him.

Sixteen years ago I was in a School of Evangelism fulfilling the obligation to meet requirements to remain on staff with Living Alternatives. My expectations were that the outreach was to be in Israel. However, God had other plans. The group felt that we were to take the musical "Heal Our Land" to the churches on the East Coast of the United States. As we individually prayed about what part God would have us play in the outreach, I felt that God said, "You will be part of Heal Our Land. This is yet another step in what I am doing with you and your singing."

We had to "try out" for the musical. When I went in to try out, my knees were shaking, but I knew that I was doing what God would have me do. I told the six musicians the story of my past musical experiences. And I said that I was there only because I believed that is where God wanted me. During the try out, one of the gals even sang with me to help me feel more comfortable!! I was placed in the alto section. I felt that it was good that I did not know any of the songs previously. This way, I would learn the alto from the beginning and let the sopranos do the melody. In the alto section was a woman who had perfect pitch and even had a degree in music. She took us aside several times a week and **trained** us. I learned how to breathe from the diaphragm, how to open my throat, how to do warm up scales. It was during this training that I thought back to that high school experience. That director knew his music. I might have had a few lessons back then and my life would have been changed for ever. However, as it was enfolding, God was the one who was getting the credit for the work that was being done in me. As we took the tour up the east coast, each performance was wonderful. Lives were touched, people were challenged, and I was humbled to think of all that God had done with my voice.

After moving to Tyler fifteen and a half years ago, I got a call from the director of the senior adult choir of the church I chose to attend. He asked me if I would join that choir. I told him briefly the story of my singing. As I was telling him, I felt that God was saying,

The Shaws Multiplied

"I am not finished with your voice. This is another step in the process I am working in you."

For two years in April, the senior adult choir made a trip to Gatlinburg, TN. to compete in the national music competition. I was a part of that. It is turning out not to be just a tour for competition; but we as a group got to minister in churches as well. It is awesome.

Pigeon Forge, TN., is right next to Gatlinburg. It is becoming a mini LasVegas with the show places. Anita Bryant, Miss America of 1958, had one of the lavish theaters there. Our choir was invited to come and sing in her program. The first half of her show is secular with good taste. The second half was all Christian and Patriotic. We were the third number in the second half. We never sounded so good. What a difference it makes to have real "state of the art" sound system and a $13 million theater that is acoustically the best!!! I felt that God was up there smiling down on us, his handiwork!!

My spirit had been broken way back there in high school. But my spirit has been freed. To some, it may sound like just a "joyful noise." But to God it is an angelic, heavenly choir.!! Hallelujah!!

So in the 16 years I have lived in Tyler, I have been so blessed to be in the church choir. I feel that my spirit sings as I join in the worshipping with the choir. Recently God reminded me of a story I heard from Mother Theresa's workers. They were attempting to bring a "throw away" woman back to some sort of healing. She had been found in a dumpster and was near death. After they did all they could to bring her some comfort, one of the workers said, "Jesus disguises himself in so many different ways." As I thought of that as I was singing in the choir one Sunday, I began to visualize each person in the congregation as having the face of Jesus. That picture has brought a whole new meaning to worshipping in song to our LORD!!!

It was my pleasure to be a part of this choir for 15 years. It has been a forerunner of the joyful noise we will be sending out when we all get to Heaven!

Doris Howe

"I love those who love me; and those who seek me early shall find me." Proverbs 8:17

"Choose you this day whom you will serve; but for me and my house, we will serve the Lord." Joshua 24:15

TESTIMONIES FROM THE DESCENDANTS

When I graduated from Arnold High School I took Normal Training classes so I could teach Country school in the state of NEBRASKA. I attended summer session each year at Kearney State Teachers College to renew my teaching certificate. In my second year of teaching at Etna school in Custer County north of Gothenburg, I met Don Peterson. He was just home from serving 2 years in the U.S. Army. Don and I stated dating and he ask me a question I had never been asked before. Don asked me if I knew Jesus as my personal savior. He questioned whether I had turned my life over to Jesus. I knew I had attended Sunday school and church but I had sinned and I needed forgiveness. So I ask Jesus to forgive me and come into my heart and life so I could live for Him. We were in North Platte visiting one of my girl friends at her church. They gave the invitation to come forward to accept Jesus. I went forward and asked Him to save me. He did. Don and I continued to date and we were married at Arnold Nebraska on May 26, 1957. We lived our married life for 55 years last May. In August Don went home to be with his Savior in heaven. I am still living for the Lord and I know I am not alone. Living without Don is difficult but Jesus is with me so I can go on each day. Blessed be the name of the Lord. Margilu Peterson"

My first year out of high school, I taught in a country school in Etna, Nebraska. In that community there was an active group of young Christians. They invited Valetta and me to join their group for fun activities. We went ice skating, and attended church Bible studies with these new friends. One evening we all went into Gothenburg to a Baptist "revival." It was there that both Valetta and I walked the aisle to accept Jesus's invitation for salvation.

When the school year ended, I went on to teach at a different country school closer to home near Arnold. We went to church quite routinely. However, my life did not show any significant changes since the Baptist experience. I went on to college full time getting my BA in 3 years and 3 summers.

From there I was to teach Jr. High English in Cheyenne, Wyoming. But during the summer before that obligation, I took a job along with several friends from college to work at Yellowstone National Park at a lunch counter. It was early in that summer work that I was swept off my feet by Joe Howe. I had no teaching about courtship and marriage God's way. So Joe and I had a whirlwind courtship that culminated in his proposing marriage. We were married in November of 1955. I broke the contract with the Cheyenne school district.

After our marriage we moved to Tucson, Arizona. My plan was to stay married till "death parted us." Long story short: My life began to fall apart with several traumatic events. It was in the midst of all of those trials, that I rededicated my entire life to Jesus. I needed help. The details are elsewhere in this book. If it had not been for the trials, I might have coasted along as a "milk toast" Christian. However, as you have read of all the wonderful ways God has used these trials to bring me to the close relationship I have with him, I hope you are encouraged. I wouldn't trade what He has made of my life for all of the riches others seek. I am content just knowing God is in control. He is God and I am not!! **Doris Howe**

When I was about ten or so, I started going to church with one of my school friends. She was Lutheran. I felt so at home in that church. I didn't know it at the time, but I feel I was getting ready to follow that faith when I got older. I'm still going to church and love it even more each day. **ERNA**

I was baptized as a child. In 1949, I confirmed my faith in the Lord at Immanuel Lutheran Church in Merna, Nebraska. I live for Jesus every day. **Detta (Shaw) Safranek:**

I was mad at a God that I didn't know. My neighbor, Sioux, came over to bring us food and tell us how sorry she was. I remember asking her how her God could allow such a thing to happen and she couldn't really answer me. For some reason, I told her that I wanted to go to her church and give "her" God a piece of my mind. She took me to a ladies get together that Chuck Smith's wife was speaking. I didn't know that it was going to be a ladies get together. I really didn't know what to expect. We got there and I remember thinking that the place was HUGE! There were so many women there. Sioux knew a lot of women as she had been a member of that church since the tent days of Calvary Chapel. We went into the big sanctuary and Kaye spoke. I don't know what she said to this day, but whatever she said was exactly what I needed to hear. At the end I had asked Sioux if she had told Kaye about what had happened to our family and if Kaye knew that I was there that day. She said, "no". So, I rudely told her that, "oh... I suppose this was just a coincidence"

Anyway, I was intrigued and hurting, so I thought that I would go on Sunday and see what "the guy" had to say. Each week, God would answer my hurts and my doubts thru Chuck's messages. I knew that Chuck was for real as he didn't jump around in the bible... . Genesis to Revelation and backed up all teachings with other teachings and didn't take things out of context! I loved it and found myself wanting to go back each week and then wanting to go on Monday nights and Wednesday nights as well.

Chuck would always say that you could go up front for prayer or questions or whatever, but I wasn't about to go up front in that huge church! Are you kidding! And, I was too much of a sinner to go up front in that beautiful sanctuary.

I went home on that one Sunday and was just thinking about all the things that I had learned and all the doubts that were answered thru Chuck's messages and thinking that maybe life with Jesus wouldn't be so bad. I was in the spare room of our house and went face down on the floor in tears. I kept asking Jesus to come into my life and save me as I had really made a mess of my life. I also asked God to take my brother to heaven as I had been having nightmares about his soul. When I got up, I felt like a huge burden had been lifted and I have been thankful ever since that moment and have been blessed with many times that God has communicated with me in one way or another! **Janet (Howe) Lopez/Lenz**

I went to Sunday school at the Baptist Church when I was in High School in Arnold, Nebraska. They had Revival Meetings that spoke to me personally. I answered that call and was baptized by emersion— the way Jesus did it in the Jordan River by John the Baptist.

Later when I came home from the Navy, Margilu and the Hunse girls were attending the Methodist Church in Arnold. It was then that I transferred my membership to the Methodist church. In College, my future wife, Shirley sang in a church choir. From the choir loft, she said she could see me and my friend, Bob McMahn, sitting in the balcony. Needless to say, I saw Shirley as well. That began a mutual attraction between Shirley and me. When cousin, Doris, introduced Shirley to me, we started attending the same church and were married there. God was involved in the preparation of that relationship even in those early years.

Years later whenever my brother-in-law, Don Peterson, and I were engaged in conversation, I could always count on his inserting the question: "Ted, tell me how you got into a relationship with Jesus." **Ted Anderson**:

"Whether I turn to the right or the left, I will hear a voice behind me saying, 'This is the way. Walk in it.'" Isaiah 30:21

"He leads me beside the still waters. He restores my soul." Psalm 23: 2-3 "I am with you, and will keep you in all places were you go." Genesis 28:15

WORLD TRAVELING

I have been a missionary for more almost 20 years. It occurred to me that before the official title, I had traveled to a few countries. As a missionary, one does not need to be on the other side of the world. I've said it more than once that I am grateful and privileged to be "stationed" in East Texas. This is a beautiful place and not a "third world" country. In preparation for what I do now, I did get to see some of the places on the other side of the world. I want to tell you a bit about those experiences.

Skiing the Matterhorn was a goal of my husband. So, we did that. It was my first time out of the country, if we don't count Mexico and Canada. I remember getting on a train after the long flight. As it would happen, I needed to look for a ladies' room. On the train, there were some, but under the seat was just a hole that opened onto the train tracks. I thought, "I'll wait until we get to the train station." Mistake. The "ladies' room at the depot was "co-educational." Picture this. It was a hole in the ground with ledges on each side for one to stand. Traveling was more comfortable with pants, so, it was pretty much impossible to straddle the "hole in the ground.' While I was trying to figure out how that was to be accomplished, a man came in and used the "hole" next to the one I was trying to master. Next time, I decided I'd take my chances with the facility in the train.

We did ski down into Italy from Switzerland. I later learned that the trail where we were attempting to ski had been used for the Olympic time trials. Needless to say, I did not look like an Olympic skier. In fact, I looked as if it was my very first time on the ski boards.

We did find an Italian restaurant right near the ski run where we went to have lunch. We Americans ordered spaghetti and red wine, of course. What else?

Going back up the backside of the Matterhorn was a breeze—in the lift. Skiing back into Zermatt was such fun. The trail was on a glacier and gentle as a lamb. That made the first half of the adventure worth it because this half was pure peace. I could ski perfectly.

When we visited Germany and France, the country side where we were was quite flat and covered with farming fields. I thought, this reminds me of the Midwest and was a confirmation of why our ancestors settled where they did in America.

Another trip took us to Scotland and England. There drivers actually drive "on the wrong side of the road.' We rented a car and began touring. It was interesting for the person sitting in the passenger's side in front. He/she was used to driving from that position. Feet were often pressed into the floor to hit imaginary brakes in that uncomfortable position as that rider could see cars coming right toward us.

In Ukraine with a missionary team, we stayed at what I called the Hotel Sputnik. I don't remember if that was its actual name, but that name suited our accommodations. There was no running water, though there was a bathroom with each bedroom. Daily we had to take buckets of water from the lower level up to our room on the second floor. This water could be heated with an electric coil, for sponge baths. It was also used to "flush" the toilet after usage.

For each meal, we would cross the "mall" and enter the back stairway to a dining room for our food. The stairway had no light. Every time I would enter that location, I would be reminded of some movie with Humphrey Bogart. I would picture him standing in that darkened location, puffing on a cigarette and saying "Here's looking at you, kid" Or "Play it again, Sam."

At the end of our stay, we had a "love feast." We invited everyone we had met during the 6 weeks we were there. That total was approximately 75. Unlike America where the rule is "One invites 100, 50 say they will come, and 25 show up." Here in Ukraine, we

The Shaws Multiplied

invited 75 and more than 85 came to the "feast." Needless to say, "FHB" got a whole new meaning, which stands for "Family Hold Back" on the food.

Another long time goal was to get to Israel. I was privileged to go with a group of students who were studying to become missionaries. We were there for three or four weeks. The Bible stories are never the same after having been right there where it all began. In addition to seeing the history unfold, we also toured the markets for bargains. I remember strolling outside some of the stores. One owner came out to greet us. Being American Tourists seemed to be written all over us. He said, "Come into my shop and I will rip you off." Evidently he had been to New York to learn the tricks of the trade.

Another "eye opener" was on a trip to China. I had been trying to put together a vacation time with some of my family. Nothing was working out. I began to pray that God would give me an answer to the dilemma. His answer was, "Call the Youth Wish A Mission base. There is always some group traveling. You do not know them now, but you will get to know them. And the schedule will work out for everyone." Sure enough, when I made the call, I had three chances to go. All three were in China. I said, "Guess I am supposed to go to China." I talked to my director about the choices. She said, go with the students. They will get to the orphanage every day. You can then get to know these kidos and bring back information and pictures. Then we will work to find families for the kids." So, that is what I did. I fell in love with those children while I was there. And some of them were then placed with families in the ministry where I am still working.

One thing I will always remember about China is that almost everyone rides a bicycle to and from work. On rainy days they all still ride their bicycles but they hold up their umbrellas as they ride. It is a beautiful colorful scene twice a day. Another thing I remember is the market. Before going, I put together my wardrobe. I had a number of denim pieces. I thought I would go to Walmart and get some denim sandals. Sure enough I got just the right pair for

$13. When I got to China's market, there were the same sandals for $3. After all, so much of what we buy in the US is made in China.

A couple of years after the China experience, I was talking to God. I said, "God, I have never been to the Southern Hemisphere. That includes Australia, South American, and Africa. Before long an opportunity opened for me to go with a group of missionaries to South Africa. That was THE best trip out of the country that I had ever taken.

Ten years before while I was on the outreach from the school, Introduction to Biblical Counseling, we did extensive studying regarding the Perfect Plumbline from the Lord. The focus for the ministry in South Africa was the Plumbline. I felt that was a "sign" that this trip was from God for me.

My work with young pregnant women made me a natural for the next event. When we visited a women's prison, there was a pregnant woman who needed prayer. It seemed that no one else was praying with her. So, I did. At another facility for young men, there were two young boys who were accused of murder. They had just met one another since coming to the facility. Since I had raised two boys, it seemed that I was drawn to minister to these two young men.

I was not involved in an actual service until scores of folks went up to the alter and were praying in the Spirit. The scripture in the Bible from the Book of Acts was so strong in my mind that I had to tell someone in the leadership. I said, "This is the Book of Acts all over again." They said, "Here, take the microphone. You need to share that message."

Altogether, I found that God used me several times. It was such a blessing to learn that God can use any of us, when we submit to His leading. I did not need to compare myself to anyone else, especially those in leadership in this ministry in which I am called and have worked for over sixteen years. We all have our individual gifts, callings, and talents. Creating uniquely is one of God's specialties.

The Shaws Multiplied

"If you will confess with your mouth Jesus is Lord, and believe in your heart that God raised him from the dead, you shall be saved."
Romans 10:9

CONCLUSION

Now we come to the last chapter of this book. But it is not the last chapter in the lives of the Shaw descendants.

As you've read the book, I've prayed that it has triggered memories from your life that you'd like to share. Some of the memories could cause us to laugh with you, cry with you, and even realize that God has worked tirelessly in your life. I pray you're blessed by those memories. They just might ignite vignettes that together could be put into Volume II of *The Shaws Multiplied*. I'm reminded of the story in the Bible of The Woman at the Well. When she met Jesus, the Messiah, who told her everything she had done, she went back to her village and told everyone about her encounter with Him. Many came back to where she'd met Jesus and personally met Him as well. Like the Woman at the Well, I've shared many of the things in my life that Jesus had a hand in. God has done many things in my life. I pray that your spirits were blessed and perhaps my times with Jesus will cause you to take a closer look at Jesus as your savior.

All of us have that heritage I mentioned in the introduction to this book. If you were to meet our ancestors today, are you certain you would join them. Is your destination with them? Jesus says, "Behold I stand at the door and knock. If anyone hears my voice and opens the door, I will come in to him and dine with him, and he with me."

What He is saying is, "I've heard the prayers of your ancestors for you all those years ago. In answer to those prayers, I want you to welcome me into your hearts and lives." You might notice on the

The Shaws Multiplied

famous picture of Jesus at the door that there is no doorknob on the outside. That indicates that you have to open the door of your heart from the inside. He is a gentleman and won't intrude uninvited, even though he is at the Father's right hand ever interceding for you. He remembers those prayers of so long ago for you.

Romans 3:23 "All have sinned and fall short of the glory of God." No prayers said in the Will of God will go unanswered no matter the time from when they were uttered until they are answered. Hold on to your hats because your life may be "fixin" (as they say in Texas meaning getting ready) for a dramatic change.

Jesus is calling. Your job is to answer His call in the affirmative. Then you, all the ancestors who have prayed for you, along with the woman at the well and me, won't be able to stop telling everyone what wonderful things Jesus did for you.

Romans 10:9-10, "If you confess with your mouth that Jesus is Lord and believe in your heart that God raised Him from the dead, you will be saved. For with the heart one believes unto righteousness and with the mouth confession is made unto salvation."

Romans 10:13, "For whoever calls on the name of the LORD shall be saved." If you feel Jesus tugging at your heart and spirit, it is because those ancestors are still praying for you. You can use these words or ones of your own. But you must pray them from your heart:

Lord Jesus, I believe You are truly the Son of God. I confess that I have sinned against You in thought, word, and deed. Please forgive all my wrongdoing, and let me live in relationship with You from now on. Come into my heart, be my Savior and my very best friend. I receive You as my personal Savior accepting the work You accomplished once and for all on the cross. Thank you for saving me. Help me to live a life that is pleasing to You. Amen.

It is simple: Christ died. He rose. He can and wants to forgive you of your sin and invite you into the Family of God. That is the message we have to share. "I have loved you with an everlasting love: therefore with loving kindness have I drawn you." Jeremiah 31:3

"There is joy in the presence of the angels of God (and praying ancestors) over one sinner who repents." Luke 15:10

Doris Howe

Now ask God to lead you to a Bible Believing-Teaching church where you can grow in this new relationship. Or if this prayer was a rededication of a time when you invited Jesus to be your Savior, but you have let yourself be caught up in the cares of this world and not taken Jesus as seriously as He would like for you to, this is also for you.

This book is a testimony of God's involvement in the lives of the descendants of Douglas and Amanda Shaw. God is the only one you can always depend on. People will disappoint you. God never will.

God made the promise sayng, "I will bless you and I will surely multiply you." Hebrews 6:13-14

Printed in the USA
CPSIA information can be obtained
at www.ICGtesting.com
LVHW061247071023
760211LV00003B/481